THE LO̶N̶ ̶̶̶̶̶̶̶̶̶̶
TO TOMORROW

Journey to the Top of the Mountain

Dear Steven,

It is never too late to be what you want to be.

May you find a word, a sentence a phrase to encourage you to never give up, no matter the challenges you face.

Scribble City
PUBLICATIONS

Acknowledgements

With the deepest gratitude I wish to thank
everyone who has impacted my life through their
presence, words, and encouragements.
You gave me strength to go from one failure to
another and never gave up. You carried me when
I could no longer carry myself.
Without you this achievement would not have
been possible.

To my precious mum who equipped me with
faith, courage, and determination.

To my three Musketeers who went through all
the storms yet never complained. You are
amazing children.
To Keith Sawyerr, whose influence has made me
a better person.

To Nicole Nelson, whose love and belief in
me gave me the strength to go through life
knowing that I am loved just the way I am.

To Lidia Perdoni whose support allowed me to
start my mobile Crêperie.

To all my friends who supported me,
I am very grateful.

To Barbara a lady of few but powerful words,
thank you very much for working on my book
with so much devotion.

CONTENTS

Introduction

As you start your adventure through this book, you will learn vital skills of perseverance, patience and most of all, faith. These skills will help you to accomplish your goals and overcome your challenges.

In this autobiography you will learn how to maintain a positive mental attitude regardless of the obstacles of life. You will be equipped with skills to manoeuvre through the different situations in your life.

You will also learn how to aim higher, keep your faith, and know that you too can overcome any challenge, and I truly mean any challenge. With God strengthening you, nothing is impossible.

My aim is for you to be empowered by my story. It may mean setting higher goals, but know that you are not alone in your struggles. There is always a way out of every situation if you keep searching, keep hoping, keep looking forward, and keep praying.

I wish to share my story hoping that somewhere, somehow, someone will be inspired by my book and be encouraged by the challenges I faced.

I hope you find great strength and comfort from reading this book.

Panic Attack   *Chapter*

1

Waking up suddenly, feeling terribly anxious, overwhelmed, distressed, I start to cry. My heart *"It is not in the stars to hold our destiny but in ourselves."*

William Shakespeare

is palpitating erratically as if it's about to jump out of my body. Trembling in my make shift bed of two mattresses stacked awkwardly on top of each other, I listen out for my children in the next room, they are bundled up in long sleeve pyjamas and jumpers; tiny bodies tightly tucked under two duvets.

I was cold and shivering. Why did you wake me up? I went to bed thinking I could sleep through you, yet here you are haunting me again. I thought I could forget for a few hours and dream, dream of a better place, dream of a house with central heating, a house where I don't have to wrap my children up in double duvets. My body is completely buried in the duvet. I can feel the icy fingers of the cold draft cruelly tickling my neck as its sharp frosty breath consumes my room. I was heartbroken. I let out a sob at the reality of our situation. The children would be awake in two hours, I was cold and didn't feel like going downstairs, but I had to. The house needs to be heated up so I must switch on the oven so we can have breakfast in a warm kitchen.

You woke me up, and now I am terrified. Terrified that this is now my reality, this is where I am in my life, I am terrified that this situation will always be my reality. God please help me, help me God, I whispered. The winter is quickly approaching, it's very cold outside. I can't go through another winter without any central heating, I was drained, I could barely get up, my muscles ached with paralysis and were giving up on me. I needed strength. Would my angel come to my rescue, would you send someone to help?

This episode of my life is one of the worst, I have hit rock bottom and couldn't possibly go any lower. I'm broke and broken. I don't have much in the fridge, no central heating, no savings and no partner. Creditors are hounding me, I barely have enough money to put petrol in the car for the school run, and no family member can afford to help me. Where do I go from here God? Where do I go from here?

Oh, finally, here you are my angel! You finally appear. Lord you have sent someone to help me! On my way back from dropping the children at school, I mentioned the issues with my heater to David. After I got home, there was a knock on my door, to my greatest amazement; there stood David with two spare heaters. Tears stung my eyes as I received the solution to ease the harsh winter cold. "Thank you, thank you, thank you." I remember blurting out over and over again.

David's arrival in my life gave me hope; it gave me the strength to press on. I had started to lose hope of a better future. He brought me two heaters, without knowing how critical my situation was. I was able to place one in my bedroom and the other in the children's bedroom. The church had also loaned us one, which was placed in the lounge. So finally this winter would be less traumatic for us. Thank you, Angel David. He helped me with the daily running around, carrying me mentally, and I felt a little bit stronger.

What an amazing feeling to finally have some support. I am so grateful for his appearance in my life. God sends people at the right time. Why him? I don't know, and I will never know, but thanks for coming to my world, thank you, I am very grateful. I felt down and was losing faith. I had stumbled and was unable to walk, but now, thanks to the support, I was able to walk again.

I was dreaming again, visualising the future I wanted to create for the children and myself. I am gradually healing from the pain of my struggle; I am building our future, working hard on the business, improving myself, investing in myself, learning as much as I can, so I will be well equipped when success comes.
Jim Rohn says *"Opportunity will pass those who are unprepared."*

Suddenly, bing, bing, I was rudely awakened from my daydream by the tormenting thought of yet another challenge, my worst nightmare.... **Child Maintenance Support.**

CMS Calls

Chapter 2

One evening in November 2015, I came home after the school run, and I saw letters piled on top *" I will prepare and some day my chance will come."* **Abraham Lincoln** of the kitchen table. I slowly picked up the CMS letter and went upstairs. Palms clammy with sweat, and heart pumping, I wondered, Lord what now? I entered my bedroom, and sank to the floor. My body convulsed and my hands shook uncontrollably as they opened the letter.

As I was reading, my heart palpitated, my thoughts in complete disarray. What next from this man? How long would this persecution go on for? What now?

My children's father was asking for maintenance for my eldest daughter who has been living with him for only a few months. I couldn't believe it. No matter how little money I had this man was determined to persecute me until he broke me...

I sat on the floor feeling completely paralyzed, and in a state of total shock. As hot tears streamed down my face I begged God to fight this battle for me, begged Him to talk to this man so he would eventually leave me alone, disappear from my life for good.

I had even wished him dead at times, his determination to destroy me was so intense, every encounter I had with him was a challenge. I prayed, and prayed, and prayed, tears are dripping down my face like an overflowing river, my body was aching with pain, both mentally and physically, and my faith was drifting I could feel my body sinking through the floor. The most painful tears were not the ones that fall from the eyes and cover the face, but the ones that fall from the heart and cover the soul. I was tired of fighting, tired of constantly defending myself, tired of being bombarded with missiles; life was already so difficult as a lone mother of three, why couldn't he just let me be and disappear forever?

I lay on my bed with the letter beside me and I prayed, God make a way, set me free from this constant persecution, please can you fight this battle for me? I have no strength left. All I am trying to do is to look after my children the best way possible, to provide a good home, equip them with the best education possible, to endow them with your words, teach them value and respect for others. Lord, I surrender all in your name, make a way where there seems to be no way.

During the weeks and months that followed, I received more and more letters, each time the letters came, I piled them up and prayed, asking God to act on my behalf.

Then one day I met a friend, and I guess the pain of all the struggle was written all over my face and when I mentioned what I was going through with the CMS she urged me to act on it by calling them. I took her advice and the next morning I decided I was going to face my fear and act.

I made a cup of tea to calm my jittery nerves and prayed. Sitting in the lounge, I finally made the call. A lady answered the phone, and after asking some security questions, she eventually transferred the call to the person dealing with my file. The lady on the other end of the line listened patiently to me. I explained how I could not afford to pay the maintenance as I barely had enough to provide for the children. I was distressed at this point, crying intermittently, I continued to narrate how on many occasions I had relied on Food Bank to provide meals for the children. I revealed to her the fact that I often gave the children only one meal because I couldn't afford more; I expressed the trenchant reality of our daily struggle.

I was paying the mortgage alone, the central heating wasn't working because I didn't have the money to fix it, I went on to tell her about my heavy outstanding credit card debt, and how my creditors were calling every day, harassing me.

I pointed out the fact that the children's father did not contribute in any form to their education, and how he did not respect the arrangement by the court which was to take the children one weekend a month, and the fact that he did not pay the correct amount for maintenance. As I opened my heart to her in the hope that they would finally leave me alone, they would finally stop this constant persecution with the endless letters and calls. Their letter was for me a form of harassment and mental torture.

As I expressed my struggles, I could hear the agony in my voice and feel the despair in my heart. The crushing sorrow in my voice and the overwhelming melancholy I felt were so deep, tears began to fall as I could no longer hold them in. As I talked to her, I felt like going in the kitchen, grabbing a knife and perforating my throat to end this agony, perhaps then, they would finally understand the emotional damage, all this was causing me.

God, you are my rescue come into my life, come and remove these suicidal thoughts from my mind. As I talked to her, I could sense from her replies that no matter what I said, no matter how I expressed my struggle, these people were determined to take from me the little I had and give to this man. It didn't matter what I told her, they still expected me to pay maintenance to him for my eldest daughter. I knew at that point it was quite hopeless carrying on with the conversation, I knew my help could only come from God, so I ended the call. I was now on my own, exhausted, deflated, discouraged, and humiliated for expressing my deep struggle to this lady who didn't have any compassion... She didn't even try to see where I was coming from or how low I felt and how depressed my soul was.

I sat on the floor in my room and cried uncontrollably. I grabbed my Bible and read Psalms 23. I read it over and over and I shouted, God please make this stop! Make this go away! Make this man stop his persecution, put an end to it, I am begging you, come to my rescue, I cannot afford a solicitor, I cannot afford mentally nor financially to take this matter to court, please God be my solicitor. Help me.

Unending Debt   Chapter
3

A few weeks later, £500 was deducted directly from my salary to pay for maintenance, leaving me with £500 for the month to pay for the mortgage, the bills, the

"A man becomes what he thinks about most of the time."

Ralph Waldo Emerson

expenses. I sat in the lounge, wondering how I was going to survive. How was I going to feed the children and pay all the bills?

My first point of action was to cry out to God, where are you? You said you would not abandon me...never forsake me, where are you?

Every day, I woke up and asked the Almighty to provide. Every day I asked Him for a miracle, and He did it. The month came to an end, and the children and I were able to eat every-day. Some friends gave me a couple of hundred pounds so I could buy some groceries. The second month another £500 was taken out. I knew then this couldn't continue, I knew something had to be done, it was two months now and the mortgage was outstanding. I couldn't pay the electricity bills, all Direct Debit came back unpaid. The bank was charging over £70 interest per month, I was overdrawn by £1500 on both my cards.

The situation was critical. I was now sinking deep into debt. God where are you? I was in this deep ocean all by myself, I had tried for so many years to swim and had just managed to keep my head above water for the 9 years I had been on my own. I had maintained the payment on the mortgage and had educated the children giving them faith but now I was going under. The water is above my head. Shortly I will drown if you don't come now. Please help! I shouted, where are You? Where the hell are you? I was scared, scared that I was going to drown in debt, scared the house would be repossessed, scared that I wouldn't be able to feed the children. Scared that I wouldn't be able to provide an education for the children. I was scared that after 9 years of battling, I would have to surrender to defeat. Lord please help me, you cannot leave me in the middle of the ocean. I am not dying here after all my efforts, I refuse to accept defeat, I refuse to fail, I refuse to fail.

I could feel the pressure, I could feel the panic. I was not able to smile as much, I was irritated and I was sure the children could feel the pressure too but I was only human. I was sorry for my little angels I never meant for our lives to turn out this way. I was sorry for not being able to provide as much as I would like to. I was sorry that they were being brought up by me alone and sorry that their dad was not involved in their upbringing as much as he could have been.

I was sorry for being a single mother. I did my very best by doing the right thing, which was to have children only when I was married, bought a house and had what society called a 'secure job'. I did everything to prevent being a single mother, but unfortunately Life had another plan for me. I was full of apologies.

I was now on my own, facing the Child Maintenance Service who, from what I could see, were determined to put us into poverty and make us homeless by deducting from my salary to give to a man who was claiming maintenance for his 16 year old daughter when he worked full time and had another job on the side. I could not possibly afford to pay maintenance. How dare such a heartless system take £500 from my British Airways salary leaving me with only £500 to live on. And because of this;

The house mortgage was unpaid.

There was no food in the fridge.

No money in my account for petrol.

I had to ashamedly rely on my son's pocket money to help.

Lord, how long are we going to struggle? What is your plan for my life?

Why are you allowing the devil to attack me? Why can't he leave me alone? All I was trying to do was to take care of my 3 children, to give them a good education and good Christian values. Why is this so difficult to understand? For the past 9 years, I have been:

Dragged to court for my son's custody.

Humiliated one winter when Father Christmas knocked at the door on Christmas day and gave the children all the expensive presents I couldn't afford. I had tried to put together a lovely meal that day, but all my efforts were in vain as the children valued the expensive presents over my little meal.

I had to surrender to the worst comments from my children for example, "You are the one who's stopping us from seeing our Dad." "You are the one who doesn't want us to go with him."

"You are the one to blame." "You are the one who's giving us pressure with education, rules, expectations, discipline."

The Last Straw

Chapter 4

For the last 3 months we had no car, except the business van. I had to take the children to school all the way to Reigate with the small van, It was an

"Whenever you think you can, or think you can't you're right"

Henri Ford

hour going and another hour to come back a total of 4 hours' drive. The van only had two seats, one for the driver and the other seat was shared between the two children, squeezed into one seat with the seat belt cutting into their shoulders. It was a painful and difficult ride for them, yet we were grateful to have the van. I was grateful that the children could somehow get to school.

Some people might see this as madness but this was the price I was prepared to pay to educate my children especially as I received tremendous support from the schools. So on that basis I was willing to play my part, and was extremely grateful to the school for helping me give my children a good education. However, the driving situation was becoming quite unbearable, my knees hurt from being bent over in such a small van for a long number of hours, the children too were getting fed up and embarrassed by this situation, they were great children but I had to admit this situation was getting to us all.

I know God you said you will not forsake me nor leave me, can you please come into my life? Can you please make a way where there seems to be no way? Can you give me the strength to overcome this new battle? Lord, with you by my side I can overcome any challenge, with you I have faith and will never go hungry, with you I will never give up hope, with you I know I can defeat the devil and all my enemies according to Mathew 21 verse 21.

My overwhelming resolution to refuse to fail was stronger than ever, but yes I am furious, yes I have tried to explain to him by letter and email that I could not afford to pay maintenance, yes his lack of acknowledgment of my letter upsets me even more, yes I feel like going to his house and creating a scene, but my senses call me back, what will I gain? My aim is to be better not bitter at the end of this battle so my only hope is you again, Lord.

I contacted my MP and arranged to see him face to face to explain the situation, and ask how he could contact the Child Maintenance Service on my behalf to request a face to face meeting. Weeks later, I was in the MP's office with my friend who came to support me, he was a lawyer but for some reason I never thought he could help because he mainly dealt with housing association properties.

Following our meeting, the MP wrote a letter to the CSM asking them to arrange a meeting and to respond to my previous letters which they never acknowledged. The CSM bureau finally replied him, but until today, are yet to reply to me directly. I had written several letters, with no reply, yet one letter from my MP and they replied promptly. How strange, is it all about power and whom you know? Not acknowledging my letters was a statement that I am not important enough to be given consideration. This lack of respect infuriated me.

Thanks to the MP's letter, the Child Maintenance Service finally decided to consider my file. I was no longer working for British Airways, therefore, they couldn't expect me to pay maintenance. The support I had received from the MP and Fred forced the CMS to finally look into the file but the issue was still not resolved. While I was not working, they couldn't expect me to pay for maintenance but my aim was to finally stop any future attempt or claim that the father might make in the future. I believed that once I started working, this nightmare of child maintenance would come to life again. The fire had been put to sleep, but not completely extinguished.

The Challenging Malaga Trip

Chapter 5

Although the children and I had a great holiday, it was an experience full of challenges. I wanted to give the children and myself a break, so I did what I

"Instead of worrying about what you cannot control, shift your energy to what you can create."

Roy T. Bennett

should never have done, paid for the holiday on a credit card, and guess what? A year later and I still hadn't cleared the balance, and the interest charges probably cost me half of the holiday price. My advice to you, please never go on holiday on a credit card, It is a trap, a costly one.

My lack of money was once again coming to haunt me even on holiday. I tried to book a theme park and other activities which required a fee but I couldn't. Luckily the hotel had a nice pool and lots of sport activities we could do at no extra cost. We booked half board so the breakfast and dinner was already paid for.

Lunch time was such a challenge. I couldn't take my babies to a restaurant, we had to manage with what we had and patiently wait for dinner, but the children were still able to enjoy the weather, the beach and the pool. A part of me was happy to see them enjoying themselves; it was a welcomed distraction to what we were going through.

After 5 days we were ready to go back, I couldn't stay any longer, and money was now becoming a real issue. I had tried to withdraw 50 Euros from the cash point, but unfortunately my request was declined because of lack of available funds. There and then I made the decision to leave on an earlier flight, luckily the nature of my job allowed me to change flights at no extra cost. The Lord was always by my side, walking with me so I could travel back to the UK. Once again thank you God for standing with me.

When we arrived at the Airport, we made our way to the train station as I couldn't afford a taxi. I stood at the station in torment not knowing how we would get home. I couldn't withdraw any money out of my Barclays account as I had already reached my maximum £1500 overdraft limit. My Santander account was no better; I could only take out £10 before I reached my £1500 maximum.

For the first time in my life I summoned up courage and asked a total stranger to lend me £5. No words can describe how humiliating this was, to be dressed beautifully and not have enough money to pay for a train fare. My body tensed as tears welled up; I blinked and fought them back. I had to try to remain strong for the sake of the children, they were watching me intently and I had to be brave, and most importantly, find a way to get home. To make matters worse, the stranger I had bravely asked had bluntly replied, "Sorry, I don't have any cash on me." I'm not sure if this was true, but I had to find another solution.

Standing at the station, I started to pray, God, help me to find a way, God give me the strength to get through this challenge, help me to get back home. I felt like crying, screaming at the world but I couldn't. I was at the platform with the children all nicely dressed with our luggage so I had to compose myself, remain focused and calm. I couldn't break down on this platform surrounded by people.

I eventually approached a ticket officer, explaining our plight, I asked if he could help with any suggestions. He advised me to buy only one child's ticket and one adult's and hopefully if there were no ticket masters I would be fine. Luckily we managed to get to

Wimbledon. Thank you God. As your word says in Deuteronomy 31:6, Be strong and courageous. Do not be afraid or terrified because of them, for the LORD your **God** goes with **you**; "He **will never leave you** nor forsake **you**." Deuteronomy 31:8, "The LORD himself goes before **you** and **will** be with **you**; He **will never leave you** nor forsake **you**."

Thank you, thank you, I am now closer to home, one more hurdle crossed, but how do I get on the bus home? I am now at the station with the children, our luggage, and one big issue. I haven't got enough money on my Oyster, I cannot pay cash so I need £5 to top up. The children are with me looking up to me to find a solution. God I am looking up to you to help me find a solution.

I was well known in Wimbledon by a few shop owners because of the mobile business I had in the area. Having traded in Wimbledon, after a while, I got to know quite a few people. Luckily I met this pleasant young man who was a shop owner and I kindly asked if he could lend me £5 because I had some issues with my card. "Sure" he quickly replied and with no hesitation he dived into his wallet and brought out a £5 note and gave it to me, which I returned the following day. A wind of relief blew over me.

I then met one of the street cleaners in Wimbledon that I was friendly with, he used to help me to set up my van, and always made sure my area was clean for me to set up. I was always very kind and respectful to him and today this paid off.

My recommendation is:
"Be nice to people on your way up because you'll meet them on your way down."

Everyone should be respected as an individual regardless of their status. As I talked to him, I explained how I needed to get on the bus so I could get home, before I even had time to go to top up my Oyster, he had approached the bus driver whom he knew, and in seconds we were on the bus, no ticket required on our way home. I was now home and the only money I had was the £5 which allowed me to buy some milk and cereal for our dinner.

Thank you Lord for blessing me even in those dark moments you always stood by me. I am very grateful to you God for making it possible to travel home from Gatwick with only £13.74.

So finally, we were home, and what an adventure! What a challenge; an unforgettable experience, a painful, shameful experience but also another lesson which adds to who I am today. As Lisa Nichols once said, "Turning your breakdowns into your breakthroughs" I was embracing this experience because I had learned another lesson in trusting God in time of struggle.

Once home, we had our dinner and we were able to sit down around the table and I talked about how life could be a challenge and how we must always aim to overcome any situation no matter what. Nothing is impossible. Yes, looking back at our journey from Gatwick home it did look as if it was impossible. Nelson Mandela once said "It always seems impossible until it's done," and I agree. The journey from Gatwick home looked undoable yet by God's grace we made it. As if this wasn't enough I was now faced with another problem, another struggle, another breakdown coming to test my faith once more.

An Unexpected Announcement

Chapter 6

As I sat around the table with the children after our light meal, heavy footsteps came thumping down the hallway and the door opened, it was my tenant.

Love yourself. It is important to stay positive because beauty comes from the inside out.

Jenn Proske

Just as I was bathing in the glory of our miraculous home coming, suddenly he barged into the lounge, announcing his intention to leave, and demanded to have his deposit there and then.

He had decided he wanted to leave that night and had been waiting for me to return to announce it. I had known he had planned on leaving, but didn't know when, and had no indication that he had planned to leave that night.

I told him that I would return his deposit within 7 days as he hadn't given me any notice, but the reply didn't go down well with him. The situation was getting out of hand as he continued to demand immediate repayment. His body language and words smacked of jealousy, because of the fact that we had been on holiday and were now unable to give him back his deposit.

As he became more and more agitated, I had no choice but to call the police to inform them of the situation and explained my intention to return his money within a week. The police logged the call and he left the next day with no deposit frothing with indignation. As I had committed, I returned his deposit the the following week using my credit card again.

Unfortunately, a year later my credit card bills still hadn't been cleared. The outstanding amount was much higher and the interest rate charged was £80 a month. Credit card companies know how to take advantage of people. I believe we are the ones who maintain these companies. The best way is to learn how to control the situation rather than let the situation control you. So, don't let the spending control you, because the only people who win are the banks, I urge you to stay away from Credit Cards if you can.

The way I handled the situation with my tenant was by remaining calm and by praying. I saw in his attitude and from his comments that he was ready for a showdown, and I knew no matter what I said he wasn't willing to listen. I could see his anger and his readiness to attack. His eyes boiled over with so much venom as he glared maliciously at me. I had stayed quiet praying in my head for God to give me the wisdom and right attitude to handle the situation. By his grace I had replied more calmly than I felt. It is amazing how the devil flees once he's lost the battle.

Proverbs 15, "A gentle answer turns away wrath, but a harsh word stirs up anger. The tongue of the wise adorns knowledge, but the mouth of the fool gushes folly."

Proverb 17:19 "Whoever loves a quarrel loves sin, whoever builds a high gate invites destruction."

I came to the realization that we learn from the challenges we face, though at the time had asked God, why me? What have I done now? I once again felt attacked. I had just managed to overcome one situation, and here I was at home safely, but Murphy's Law had to visit me.

I had learned the hard way to manage tenants' deposits better, and to protect myself, I didn't take it out knowing I couldn't pay back once I used it.

So, the lesson which I learnt and would like to pass on to you is to remain calm in any situation you are facing. Trust God and He will put the correct words in your mouth. Be wise in the way you speak. **Proverbs 16:32, "Whoever is slow to anger is better than the mighty, and he who rules his spirit than he who takes a city."** Better to be patient than powerful, better to have self-control than to conquer a city.

The Power of Words Chapter 7

Words have amazing power. *"The Lord GOD gave me the ability to teach so that I know what to say to make the weak strong."*

Words can change a life, inspire a nation.

Words can mend a broken heart. *Isaiah 50:4*

Words can make this world a beautiful place, but words can also speak venom.

Words have destroying power and can be poison for those who are affected by them.

My routine every day was that I woke up at 5:30 am, prayed and then had a short read of my Bible. I woke the children up at 6am and by 7am I start the school run.

Sometimes on the way back, I stopped over at McDonald's for a hot chocolate. I would read for an hour, or reply to some emails, before I set off to the gym for another hour and eventually started my working day between 9:30 to 10am.

As I walk into McDonald's I am regularly welcomed by the staff with a warm and friendly "hello." From their body language, their smiles, and words, I could see they had a lot of respect for me. I guess my polite attitude, the way I walked and the way I was dressed helped attract respect.

Theresa, who cleaned the lobby would always like to come to me and have a few minutes' chat.

"Hello Madam how are you today?" "Are you going to do your office work?" she would ask politely. I would then take off my headphones to give her my full attention, and ask her how the previous day's work had been, and what time she would finish today. Our conversation usually lasted 5 to10 minutes, and after this she would often say, "Ok, I will leave you to continue your work." I could read from her attitude that she regarded me as a chief executive, a boss Madam, I could read her mind. Her face beamed what she was thinking, "I have a lot of respect and admiration for you." Although I was only in McDonald's I must admit it was a great feeling to have the respect of others. I felt blessed and grateful for the attention and respect I received.

I visualised how it would be to own my own company and have my staff welcome me in such a manner, and to be an encouragement to those around me.

It was a wonderful feeling to be respected. It encouraged me to continue to work hard, to continue to face the challenges in my life and most importantly it gave me hope, hope to change my life around, hope to achieve my goals, hope to continue to love and care for others, hope to love and to be loved. And, yes, words matter. They may reflect reality, but they also have the power to change reality and the power to uplift and unfortunately to also abase.

But sadly something unexpected happened which forever changed the warm and genuine welcome I had become accustomed to.

On this particular Monday morning, I walked in and received the normal, "Hello how are you today?" I returned the greeting in my usual friendly manner and ordered my usual hot chocolate and took my seat. A few minutes later Theresa came for her usual chat and as she approached I could smell an extremely overpowering and unpleasant putrid smell coming from her and the clothes she was wearing as if there was a dead rat hanging around her. The smell was so repulsive I couldn't concentrate on the conversation so I asked myself if I were in her position would I want people to make me aware of it, or would I prefer them to comment behind my back? For a few minutes I debated in my mind, wondering if it was my place to tell her, unsure of what to do.

My response was, I'd rather know so I would do something about it.

Being such a delicate subject, at this point I was feeling quite uncomfortable, petrified even. I didn't want to upset her as she was a very nice lady and I certainly didn't want to damage our cordial relationship. I called her again and started with a question.

"Have you been working for long, what time did you start?" She replied "Only a few hours." I then carefully made allusion, hesitating slightly, I quietly said "Oh I don't know if you are aware but there is a very strong odour coming from your clothes, are you aware of it?"

Suddenly, in that moment everything changed. In those few seconds her facial expression altered. She no longer wanted to talk, in those few seconds she had made her decision and walked away upset, in those few seconds the overwhelming respect she had for me was damaged for ever. I sat there feeling so embarrassed. Did I do the right thing?

Would it have been better if I had kept it to myself? I was so sorry but my intention had been to help and not to hurt.

Words, can be powerful, choose them right, to build and not destroy.

Have you ever been in a situation like this? Have you ever hurt someone with your words that no matter what you said or did you could never make it right again?

Just like a broken vase, once it reaches the floor it shatters in pieces and can never be the same again. Yes of course you can put the pieces back together, but regardless of how well you put it back it will never be as perfect again.

I advise you to be extremely careful with your words and avoid making the same mistakes that I made.
When you speak to your children, your spouse your friends, your colleagues, or your boss choose your words carefully.

The power of words is immense so use it to empower people.

Weeks following the incident with Theresa, I went into the same McDonald's and everything had changed. Suddenly I no longer felt welcomed. I felt uncomfortable as hostile eyes watched me, my conscience began playing games with me trying to make me feel guilty, with accusing thoughts of, "You are not a nice person, you shouldn't have mentioned it to her." Negative thoughts had now taken over and although I fought desperately to remain positive, the accusations in my mind had over powered me. As I tried to read, the negative thoughts flooded in stealing my concentration, my tranquillity, and my peace of mind.

So, I decided to act, I decided that I was going to find a way to make amends. At least if I could mend it by half it would be better than nothing.

My Penance

I had her in mind, so I walked into a shop one morning and bought a pretty card. The inside was blank.

"Your beliefs become your thoughts, Your thoughts become your words, Your words become your actions, Your actions become your habits, Your habits become your values, Your values become your destiny."

Mahatma Gandhi

I got home, and sitting on the dining table pen in hand, I thought for a long time on how to express my feelings, then I began to write....

Dear Theresa,

I am taking the time to write you this card to apologize for the hurt I caused. My intention was to help, not to hurt you.

I had asked myself would I prefer that someone mentioned it to me or have them talk behind my back? So I made the decision based on what I would prefer, and I am sorry.

You are a very nice lady with excellent customer service skills and I truly hope this incident wouldn't change the fantastic service you give.
Once again, my apologies.
I wish you the very best,

Warm regards

Few days later, I did my usual stop and handed the card to her manager who in turn handed it to her. I had ordered my hot chocolate and took my seat with my book and laptop.

Obviously, this was on my mind so I wasn't 100% concentrating on my reading, but I still carried on reading. 10 minutes later she comes over, her facial expression was slightly more at ease, and she had made the decision to forgive me although she was still upset but clearly more willing to forgive. Then she comes over and brings a little gift as a sign to say thank you for the card. She hands me a little sticker knowing that I usually collected them so I could get a free hot chocolate after 6 stickers. Although it was only a sticker, to me this represented so much more. It was a sign that said thank you for your card, thank you for making the effort to say sorry. Her sticker made me feel forgiven and I felt great, I felt a weight off my heart, I felt so much better, happier, and grateful for her forgiveness.

Few minutes later, she brings a full coffee, milk, spoon, and sugar. I knew then that the vase that shattered on the floor was put back together, although it would never be perfect, it would be ok. Ok was enough to move on with.

I was delighted that somehow I could use my words to build and empower her, I was able to use my words wisely and powerfully. I learnt a significant lesson from this.

However, from that moment onwards I knew it was time to move on, I had been taught a great lesson. It was a shame that I had to experience it this way, but I guess it's all part of our learning curve in life.

I knew I would never feel the same again in this McDonald's so I made the decision to move to another and embrace what I had learnt; Once again life had equipped me with a new experience.

The Next Meal

Chapter 9

I woke up in the morning feeling anxious again, my body was feeling tense. My heart was racing with fear, I

> "There is no man living that can not do more than he thinks he can."
> **Henry Ford**

started to cry under the weight of the anxiety attack. I tried not to show it to the children but I was afraid that again I wouldn't be able to afford my next meal, afraid that again I wouldn't be able to feed them, afraid that we would sink deeper into this ocean of darkness.

It was Sunday. I pondered whether to go to church, perhaps I would find someone to help me, then again, I could just stay at home. I was feeling ashamed. It had become embarrassing. How was I going to ask for help? How was I going to explain to someone that although we looked great and were elegantly dressed, and didn't appear as if we were struggling, we had no food in the fridge and no petrol in the car? How could I tell them that I couldn't go to the cash point because I had reached my maximum overdraft limit on all my accounts? How could I justify my situation? My heart, my head is tormented. What should I do Lord? In **Deuteronomy 31:6** You said **"Be strong and courageous. Do not fear or be in dread of them, for it is the Lord your God who goes with you. He will not fail you nor forsake you."**

I finally made the decision to go to church, I believed that even if I couldn't afford my next meal, at least I would hear a words of encouragement. I would sing, pray and rejoice with others which would be far better than staying at home alone with my struggles.

The children were in the car. I looked at the red light on my dashboard which showed I was low on petrol, and desperately hoped the car would reach church and not stop on the way, and yes it didn't stop.

I was in church seated beside the children and enjoying the sermon. A thought came to my mind, perhaps I should go up to the front and express my difficulty, but I quickly recoiled at the thought. I didn't want to be judged, I didn't want others to think how someone that looked so charming did not have even the basic needs like food. How could a glamorous model not have any pennies in her pocket? When I had walked in earlier I was greeted by the Host Team and the first comment she had made was, "How is the lovely model today?" So, I couldn't dare share my struggles, I couldn't let her know that the lovely model had absolutely nothing. I didn't have the courage.

The Lord knew and so, eventually I was able to approach someone, knowing that I could trust the person, and I quietly asked him what he had planned for lunch and if I could ask him for a favour. Could he invite us for lunch? And with no hesitation he invited us all.

Thank you, God, you have made a way for us again, thank you because you say you will not leave me, thank you because you always provide for us and I am very grateful.

Before we left church, I approached a lady who managed the Food Bank and within a second she invited me upstairs for a few minutes, it was quiet and discreet. She handed me a few coupons which would allow me to feed the children during the week of their holidays. I was very grateful for her discretion and her encouragement.

Once again, thank you Lord, you always make a way for us. Thank you Lord, with you I can overcome any challenges, with God's strength I could do and overcome anything and you can also. Believe me, if I did, so can you. I am not stronger than you, I promise you, you can look up to Him.

Our Sunday lunch was very nice, we received a warm welcome, we all felt very comfortable and most of all I wasn't judged by my appearance. I was loved and welcomed. We had a fantastic day and were grateful for the beautiful lunch and the beautiful day we had.

Sometimes the best things we can do is not to think, not to wonder, not to imagine. Just breathe and have faith that everything will work out for the best.

Ask and it Will
Be Given to You

Chapter
10

I woke up one morning, I hadn't looked at the time but I believe it was around 4am. Wondering once again how I was going to feed the children during this school holiday.

Everything happens for a reason, my past story was preparing me for today."

Carole

My heart was palpitating; and my brain was working overtime asking me how I was going to survive. Suddenly I reached for my Bible, opened it and started to read Psalms 37 repeatedly until the words penetrated my conscious and subconscious. I read the verse until my anxiety disappeared. Verse 3 said **"Trust in the Lord"** which I was trying to do but I must admit it was very difficult. I was trying to focus on God's word but my negative thoughts were trying to overtake my positive thoughts. It took a great deal of effort to fight it.

The negative thoughts kept telling me:

You could barely pay for your train journey last night to attend your Toastmaster Club.

You were hungry and you couldn't afford to buy a snack.

Your house hasn't been paid for in over 2 months now.

Your son's school fees is outstanding and although the school covered most, however you still can't cover the minimum amount they are charging you.

Water bills are outstanding by over £800.

You have less than £2 in your overdraft account.

You need petrol to take your daughter to school tomorrow morning.

Your son's school dinner account needs to be topped up, otherwise he won't have any lunch.

You would like to repair your house before you can put it on the market for sale but you need money for all the repairs, so where will you find it?

Your aim was to move closer to the school to avoid the 4 hour drive every day.

So how on earth are you going to do all this? How are you going to come out of this dark place? Who will help you based on the fact that you don't have a husband, you don't have any family member in this country or anyone to support you. Your family's financial situation is very similar, maybe not as dire as yours but they certainly can't afford to help you. You can't even ask your children's father, you already know the answer. You already know this man has no genuine heart to help, so you are on your own. The negative thoughts left me in complete despair.

Lord you said in **Luke 11:9 "Ask and it will be given to you"**, Lord you said

"Seek and you will find, Knock and the door will be opened for you, for everyone that asks receives and everyone that searches finds and everyone who knocks the door will eventually open."

So, I am asking you Lord to transform our lives. Remove me from this house before the government takes it from us. I want to achieve great things. I HAVE BIG DREAMS.

I am asking you Lord to provide a big house, a fantastic house for us in Reigate. Increase my salary to a minimum of £100 000 a year.

Lord I am asking for beautiful holidays at least twice a year.

I am asking for a successful business.

I am asking for an amazing talented, ambitious, driven, sporty husband.

I am asking for a total transformation of my life and the children's lives.

I presented my request fervently trusting Him to help me achieve them.

Someone at the Door

Chapter
11

I was home alone, the children were with their father for two days. I woke up and did my reading; I loved the book I was reading by Joyce Meyer, "The battlefield of the mind". I strongly recommend it! So, I was enjoying the fact that I didn't have anyone to look after apart from myself, it was a "Moi Temps". I felt a great sense of happiness and relief. Relieved that I didn't have to be a mother today, relieved that I could be me and be myself. Today, I could do what I liked to do, it was a golden time. Sometimes I missed just being me, I missed my own company, so today was my day, I was determined to enjoy it and make the most of it.

"Silence is the best answer to anger."

Gandhi

Knock, knock, knock, I wondered who that could be, I wasn't expecting anyone.

Hurriedly, I wrapped myself in my dressing grown and rushed to the door, and to my surprise it was my son. He had finished his football practice and been driven all the way back by his father just to ask me for £10 to go to the barber's for a haircut.

On hearing this, I felt paralyzed, my legs and entire body felt weak, I could barely stand. I was shocked and dumbfounded. I could feel the hair on the back of my neck standing up.

How could a father who drove a Mercedes Benz bring his own son all the way back home just to ask for £10 from a mother who barely had enough to eat that day? How could a father stoop so low?

I prayed, Lord help me. Help me to deal with this unexpected attack. Help me to be strong, help me to remain calm. All

I wanted to do was to come out of the house and break him and his car into pieces. I felt like screaming. I felt the pain in my chest, my instincts told me to go out there and insult him. Go out there and smash him and his shiny car in pieces. Lord please help me, help me to deal with my son who's in front of me, feeling terribly hurt by this situation, I pleaded.

I was so sorry for him, I was so sorry that he, a young boy had to experience this. I had done everything I could for him to have a good childhood, and I was sorry I had to be a single mother, sorry for failing him as a parent.

Just before he came, I had been having a pleasant time by myself. Just before he came, I was enjoying a moment of happiness. Just before he came I was able to put all my bills on hold, the school fees, the outstanding school dinner money, the school trip money, mortgage house bills, credit card bills etc.

I was even able to block out the sound of my creditors calling me.

Why did this man deliberately want to disturb my peace? Lord give me the wisdom to deal with my little angel who was standing uncomfortably in front of me, feeling as miserable as I was. So, I gently told him to go back to the car and tell his father that I did not have the £10.

As my son left, I felt as if I had been shattered into pieces, and I had to rebuild myself and go and find my peace again. I had to go and find strength in my inner mind, body and soul, I had to kneel down and beg God to bring back my peace. My anger didn't want to submit, it refused to kneel, my anger was so strong that I had to battle and battle until finally the anger surrendered, although it wasn't easy.

Eventually, I felt a lot better and able to continue my day, but I must admit it was extremely difficult to find peace. I was so upset by such a malicious action, I was still in shock. I repeated the sentence

"With God on my side I can overcome
any challenge, I mean any challenge",
over and over again until the rage left me.
I was able to find peace again and
determined not to sink lower than this.

My Vision Chapter
12

I woke up feeling overwhelmed by my desire to turn my life around. I felt the urge to improve my life.

This vision message is a witness pointing to what's coming. It aches for the coming–it can hardly wait! "

Hab 2:2 Message

I found myself at a crossroads. As I looked to the left, I could see bills, and as I looked to the right I could see overdrawn accounts. I had nearly reached my Santander overdraft limit by £10, the Lloyds account had only £5 while the Barclays account had already reached its overdraft limit. As I looked ahead, I could see the goals I had set for myself and my children.

My desire was to set up a Creperie-Guadeloupe Restaurant Bar and to have a beautiful home. My house would have amazing views, green landscape surrounds and a breathtaking garden. The inside would be modern, clear, beautiful and spacious but very cozy.

I was looking ahead and I saw the great education I wanted to provide for my children, I could see us having two or more amazing holidays each year.

As I looked ahead, I could see myself driving my own car, and having a very good standard of living. I could see all the people I could help spiritually and financially, all the people I could motivate, encourage, and empower. My struggles could help others.

I could see the desire of my heart which is to be a blessing to my children and to all the people who would happen to cross my path.

I could see a life of abundance, in my family, my professional and spiritual life.

I am grateful to God, and all the people who played a part, be it big or small in my story. All the people who lifted me when I needed help. All the people from the Food Bank who provided me with a meal when I had nothing to eat. All the people who gave me money when I didn't have a penny, I am so grateful to you all. Thank you, thank you for coming into my life, thank you for your support. I am very grateful to you all. May God bless you all.

Looking ahead, I could see myself proud of the woman I had become:

A woman who walks by faith, and not by sight. Who faces the future with boldness and enthusiasm.

A woman of value, disciplined consistent and persistent.

A woman who is responsible, dependable, enthusiastic and energetic.

A woman who is passionate with the life of God pulsating through her.

A woman of vision, who could see the invisible and do the impossible.

A woman of value. I am a masterpiece, a miracle, uniquely fashioned by God.

A woman of class and elegance, beautiful within and without.

A woman of persistence who was born to win, designed for accomplishments, engineered for success and endowed with the seeds of greatness.

A woman of strength, who recognizes and releases the sparkle, color, beauty, joy, and laughter that is within her.

A woman who cares and loves you, and wants you to find yourself in these words.

A woman who wants to touch your heart and give you hope that everything is possible for those who believe.

This is what I see when I look ahead.

Looking Back   *Chapter*
                                   13

I look back, and see a
place I don't want to go
back to. I see a place that
equipped me with all the
skills I now have, but a
place which belongs to
my past, a past I don't

*"The secret of success is
learning how to use
pain and pleasure
instead of having pain
and pleasure use you. If
you do that, you're in
control of your life. If
you don't, life controls
you."*

Tony Robbins

want to repeat. In this place, I see:

Myself driving to the Food bank
feeling humiliated, broke and broken, my
heart pumping, my head asking why am I
in this situation? Is this my reality? How
did I create this? How did I fail my
children in such a way? I see myself
arriving at the reception feeling so broken
inside, but also grateful that some people

cared enough to provide for us. I'm waiting outside while the lady is gathering the grocery, my book in my hand reading the "Power of Thinking Big" by David Schwartz, crying but refusing to let the tears drop, refusing to show how broken I was, how humiliated I felt inside. I am praying asking God to transform my life, begging and begging and begging. Lord, please transform our lives!

I am driving the children to school and wondering if I will have enough petrol to drive back, knowing that I don't have money, I am worried, Lord please help me to drive back and make a way for me to collect them later. Provide for us, and He did, through a friend who gave me petrol money. I see myself going to Tesco and shopping for less than £10 wondering if the card would go through, praying that it goes through to save me the embarrassment, the humiliation. I don't want to pretend again that I forgot my pin. I am angry at myself, angry that I allowed myself to sink so low that I couldn't even buy £10 worth of groceries.

I see myself taking the children to McDonalds for a small treat and wondering if I will have enough money. I did have just enough, £6.50 to be exact. I see myself sitting down and looking at the children and feeling so overwhelmed. I see myself going to London one day and taking the children for a treat, they were shocked and then their faces lit up in excitement as I offered to take them to dinner. I can hear them asking, "Are you sure mummy?" With their little angelic faces, looking at me and wondering whether we could afford it. I was quite touched by their comments; the expression on their faces will forever be engraved in my mind. I felt like crying but I had to compose myself and put on a smile.

Life was such a struggle, I could barely afford any groceries as we had been forced into poverty after the CMS deducted half of my salary. There was no reason to continue to work, I was now struggling to pay for the children's schooling, my salary was no longer enough to live on, and to hold a job. Seeing as the system had demanded that I pay maintenance, after a long deliberation I made the decision to finally stop flying.

Motherhood *Chapter*
14

Here I was, a lone mother, trying her utmost to provide for her children, doing her very best to look after and give

"A man must be big enough to admit his mistakes, smart enough to profit from them, and strong enough to correct them"

John C Maxwell

them a good education at the same time, trying to be both a father and a mother to them. Unfortunately the system supposed to offer such support on the contrary, allowed this man to persecute me, and throw us into poverty and torment us. I felt broken, completely distressed.

The system CSA, CMS failed us, refusing to see that this man who was asking for maintenance didn't even pay any maintenance for the other two children.

How could a system which was supposed to be in place to protect mothers like myself put us in poverty? How could they not see the reality of the situation? Were they blind and oblivious to this man's nastiness? What would it have taken for someone to hear my cry?

I tried to make this man understand that all I was doing was for the benefit of the children. I had written countless emails and letters trying to make him understand that my concern was the children.

I tried to encourage him to be part of the children's daily lives, to take an interest in their schooling, take our son for football practice, or even take part in the school run, but he didn't respond. I finally had to accept and deal with the fact that he didn't want to be part of their daily lives. I had to accept that I would have no support from him. I was on my own and this was the harsh reality to accept. I had to accept the fact that he would never be a supportive father instead he would do his best to make my life as difficult as possible.

With this realization I turned to my only help, God.

I look back and see the resilience to succeed no matter what. I look back and I accept the past but refuse to let this past dictate my future. I look back and I see a situation that I no longer want to be in.

I look back and say thank you, past, but you do not define me.

I look back and say my future is ahead of me.

I look back and say I want this past to make me stronger.

I promise you if you stay positive you will overcome those challenges. But remember be better not bitter.

I look back and I am grateful to God that I survived all the turbulence of life.

I look back and I thank my past for shaping me to the woman I am now.

I look back and say goodbye to my past and embrace my future.

This is all I see when I look back and I certainly don't want to look back or go back to the past. I choose to forget the past and not focus on it otherwise I will miss my future. I aim to drive looking forwards not backwards. My future is ahead and I am looking forward to it.

I urge you to look forward, not backward, I urge you to drive looking forward and not drive looking at the rear view mirror. I urge you to press on, because where you are now, you are not there to stay, something better is ahead.

I know and I understand it can be difficult for you to press on, it can be difficult for you to see past all the struggles that you are going through, but believe me, I have been there. If you press on you will win.

Always look ahead, remember to smile no matter what, at times it may seem impossible to smile but don't lose your smile, think positive, stay positive.

Everything is controlled by your mind, smile and keep moving forward.

You are stronger than you think, though you may not see it right now, believe me, you can overcome any challenge with God's strength.

You will win if you keep a positive mindset, you will conquer whatever you are facing right now. Remember God is with you, He will give you strength if you believe in him, and believe in yourself, and you will overcome this struggle because you are powerful. Don't ever let any situation or people make you think that you are not. Believe, believe, believe and you will succeed. You were born to win, born and designed for success, you are a masterpiece don't you ever forget that.

About to Surrender   Chapter
                                        15

There was this time in
my journey I nearly
forgot who I was. I got
ready to go out like
always, dressing up very smartly because
this was my only force, it was my only way
of staying alive. I looked in the mirror,
and suddenly I got sick of my reality. I got
sick of looking at this gorgeous looking
and elegantly dressed model before me, I
looked like an expensive chic, but didn't
have any penny in my pocket, didn't have
any money in my bank account. I recoiled
at the lovely face, the beautifully dressed
image staring back at me. I was sick at the
sight of my own image. The negative
voice inside of me began telling me, why
do you bother? Why do you look so nice

"Tough times never last, but tough people do."
Robert Scheller

when you know you have no money in your pocket and the bank? I couldn't face my reflection as the negative voice continued to bombard me. Why do you keep on dressing up? Why do you keep on trying to look the part, why? Why? It mocked. You know you've got nothing in your bank account so dress like someone who has nothing in their account. Why are you fighting to keep your appearance and dignity? Give it up! Surrender! You are poor, so dress, talk and think like the poor person you are.

I was fighting. This was my last card. God if I surrender to this negative voice, then what? I would lose the game completely. If I surrendered my last card then I would be out, give up and life would beat me. I cannot, I cannot, because as long as I've got my last card I can still win, I can still come up and face the world. I was presentable, elegant, chic, and I could still attract people to help me. I could still go to meet people like MP's, go to expensive bars, have coffee in beautiful places such as Hotel Café Royal, Bingham Restaurant Richmond, Sarastro in London. I was still able to go to places like the Jumeirah Hotel in London and meet people. I can still fight the game of life, I can still WIN, I can still surround myself with classy and chic people, I can surround myself with the people I want to be like. I know if I surround myself with business people, chic ladies and gentleman who are fighters I will eventually be one. I know this is where I want to be at, and I know if I surrender now I will lose all my chances to ever be there. If I give up my last card, the game is over. I would have lost. I was determined to follow Iyanla Vanzat's advice. I refused to fail, I refused to fail, I just refused to fail.

I am not going to give in, Lord hold my hand, help me to dress up, help me to overlook my finances and focus on who I am on the inside, who I have always known myself to be. Help me to remember my destination and my goals, help me to rise above the fact that my bank account doesn't match my goal and how I look. Lack of money shouldn't make me surrender to who I am not. My bank account does not determine who I am.

Help me to carry on dressing up, standing up to life, help me to still look the part no matter what, and open doors for me to meet successful people who refuse to give up on life, people who look the part. Lord give me the strength, determination, perseverance to hold on, and never ever give up on my last card. I believe this card is able to take me to the top, this card, although it's the only one card left, will help me to win, and it's enough to finally make it.
I am holding on to you, so now let's go. I am ready to face the outside world.

After I had encouraged myself, all the negativity was replaced with positive encouragement. Let's go, chic and elegant lady, you look the part, let's go and see what life has in store for you. Expect to win. Expect good things to happen to you and I promise you, eventually they will.

God's blessing comes in many forms and this is one of them...

Flight to Geneva

Chapter
16

I was on a flight to Geneva, welcoming my guests with a warm smile. One

> *"Through hard work, perseverance and a faith in God, you can live your dreams."*
>
> *Ben Carson*

of my passengers sitting in 1A was very kind and pleasant, so we started talking about business. While we were talking, I found out what he did for a living and also shared my ambition and dream to open my very own Creperie-Guadeloupe Restaurant Bar.

During the flight, we engaged in a long conversation and I was interested to know how he reached that level of success. During our conversation, I also mentioned that I was looking to buy a Coffee Machine for my Creperie and to my amazement, one of his close friends had a business selling Coffee machines, he put me in touch with him via email, and before I knew it, the coffee machine which cost over £5000 had been paid for and delivered at my door step. I was even more amazed to know that this gift didn't come with any expectation of a date or anything else; it was simply a gift from the heart.

Sometimes you might think God is no longer there, sometimes you might think you will never overcome your challenges, you might think there is no good person in this world, everyone is against you and nothing is working, but my advice to you is look up, smile big, be open and kind to others and they will also be kind and open towards you. But you must step forward first.

Force yourself to smile, because when you do it opens doors to others to smile back, as you may know, the human mind is built with Mirror Neurons, and we tend to mimic the smiles or frowns of others because it helps us to better understand what other people are feeling, allowing us to respond appropriately.

Smile and life will smile at you. Think positive and smile even if you don't feel like it.

I urge you to open the door to greatness with a smile.

Thanks to my smile I could connect with so many people, exchange a kind word, an experience, a contact detail, a destination, a warm hug, or the name of a place.

A tip on how to do something better; My smile has captivated so many people and my aim is to continue, someone once told me "Never let anything or anyone take away your beautiful smile." That comment has always stayed with me.

'As Maya Angelou once said:
"I've learned that people will forget what you said, people will forget what you did, but people will never forget how you made them feel." And this person's remark on my smile was enough to get me through the storm in my life.

Try to Save It

Chapter 17

[My journey through divorce and why you should try your very best to save your marriage if possible.]

It was Easter Sunday, the children were with their father, and I was on my way to church. I

> "Many a man has a treasure in his hoard that he knows not the worth of."
>
> *J.R.R. Tolkien*

was in church listening to the sermon and I suddenly visualized the reason God created family and why a parent's union is the base for a family.

I realized my family was broken, and so was my dream to have my children and spouse around me. I realized the damage of divorce and the loneliness that comes with it. The feeling of not belonging to a union, to a close family, a bubble, a precious bubble where you feel safe to be yourself.

I realized how this can affect everyone, especially if there was no communication between the parents.

I had on countless occasions tried to keep an amicable relationship with their father, and made numerous attempts to involve him in the children's daily lives, asking for support with their education. A number of times, I had mentioned how difficult it was bringing up 3 children with no family member in the UK and had literally begged him for help. I then finally made the decision to stop asking and stop any further damaging communications. I didn't want any more confrontations and pointless conversation.

Often people will notice the change in your attitude but little will they realize it was their behavior that made you change towards them.

Always be more concerned with what God thinks about you than what people think about you.

I learned that a man's background has a huge influence on his behavior.

My recommendation is:
Before you partner with someone,
check his family background
and his values.

This will have a huge impact on your life together. We all know when love comes knocking, our sense of reasoning goes through the window, we become blinded by our feelings.

John once told me, "My mum looked after two children alone, so why can't you look after your three." From this statement, I knew that no matter what I did or said he wasn't going to get involved in the children's education because of what was engraved in him.

Until today John still can not see the reason his contribution is important, neither can he understand why he needs to help financially, nor why he should look after the children more than once a month. He does not understand why he should take up his responsibility as a father, nor why I want him to be a role model for his children. Even now, he still doesn't agree with the court's decision for us to remain in the house. As far as he was concerned, the government should re-house us. I recall a conversation in which he adamantly stated "We sell the house, I get my share and the government will house you all." He was completely clueless to his responsibility as a parent, and to try to change such a mindset was impossible. Unless they are willing to change by themselves, there is really nothing one can do except pray.

The Rough Road to Divorce

Chapter 18

The road to divorce was so incalculably much worse than what took us there in the first place.

"You will face many defeats in your life but never let yourself be defeated."

Maya Angelou

The problems, difficulties and constant persecutions were so much worse than the issues we had while still married.

Often we think divorce is a way out, not knowing that it can be an unending nightmare. I understand that for some of us divorce was the best option, but for the majority, post-divorce stress was worse than all the years spent together. The wrangling over financial settlement and the pain caused to the children, the constant back and forth in court, the stress, the overwhelming desire for revenge and constant tirade of abuse. I can honestly admit that the post-divorce was a living hell.

It was 4 am and I had just woken up shivering with the pain of the reality of my divorce. I could feel the devil next to me, waiting to take my soul, and I was frantically fighting, fighting to stay positive and call on my Lord. I was fighting for my life, to stay mentally fit and not lose my mind.

I had woken up to my nightmare, and I could see myself ending in a psychiatric hospital. I saw my image in the mirror, and I had lost a tremendous amount of weight. I couldn't believe how gaunt I had become. What had happened to me and how did I get to this? I was scared, so scared I couldn't even talk to my relatives, this must be a horrible nightmare. I frantically went on the floor and started to do sit ups. It was 4 am and one might think I was already crazy, but I knew it was just a way to keep my sanity because I knew once the Devil possessed my mind, then he would have a complete hold on me. So, there I was on the floor doing sit ups to preserve my mind. I had to survive, I had to escape this nightmare and make sure it never became my reality I desperately needed to work on my mind. I forced myself to stay positive, to call on my Lord. Save me Lord! Save me! Help me to out of this nightmare. Help me to keep my mind and to stay in control. I now understood, I could see why many people go crazy and end up in mental institutes. It could happen to any of us, regardless of race, background, age, or status. Your mind is a precious gift given by God. You must guard it, protect it.

I had only visualized it and seen myself there. The human mind can be so fragile and also so powerful; I now understood the power of the mind. I understood why everything begins in the mind and I could see why the devil wants to attack our mind, because once he controls our mind then our body would surrender.

I had to keep busy to preserve my sanity and stay positive. It was a matter of life and death. I had to escape the negative thinking so I did everything I could. I joined the gym, I worked, I continued to focus on the children and on my goal which was very difficult at times, because sometimes, I thought I would never make it to the other side of the river but eventually I did, because I AM THE MASTER OF MY THOUGHTS.

> ### My recommendation is:
> *Do whatever you can to guard your mind. If this means walking in the park, joining a gym or going out, or even travelling, becoming a workaholic, changing house or joining a dance club, do it.*

Whatever you do, please find a way to stay busy when you find yourself in a difficult situation, do it and I promise you, you will win.

George Bernard Shaw was right. He summed it all up when he said:

"The secret of being miserable is to have the leisure to bother about whether you are happy or not", so if you are going through a storm just keep busy, lose yourself in action.

January 2008
Quit Notice

Chapter
19

I had been fighting to keep a roof over our head. His determination to sell was stronger than his love for the children,

"Success is the ability to go from one failure to another with no loss of enthusiasm."

Winston Churchill

or even the understanding that we needed a roof over our heads. He couldn't see our needs, his only thought was, "I need my money and I'm out, I don't care where you all stay, just give me my money." So, I was going through hell trying to convince him and the judge that I couldn't afford a place on my part-time contract with British Airways.

John's harassment was so strong that I was losing faith. My strength to fight was weakened, but eventually I found a lawyer who was extremely kind and willing to help. Mr. P wrote a letter to his solicitors stating that as long as I have the children in full time education I was under no obligation to leave the house. The letter was enough to force John to realize that the house wasn't for sale.

I couldn't afford to buy him out, so the judge secured his share (his asking price) of the house.

His share was increasing in interest as the years went by. John had not contributed to the mortgage payment for over 10 years yet he would still be entitled to the interest made through the years which would triple his share. I saw his share as a safe investment, the longer I remained in the property and paid the mortgage the higher his return was with no financial contribution on his part.

Looking back, I would have preferred to have been able to buy him out because the constant harassment we endured because of this property was horrendous.

At every opportunity, I was reminded that I was the one who had the house, though he didn't pay a penny. Although I had tried to make him understand that his part of the deal wasn't bad because if I stayed, his share increased without his contribution, but he couldn't see that. His only focus was that I got the house and I was living in it. The children's welfare didn't matter.

Because of this resentment and constant persecution, I had been trying to sell the property for the past 8 years hoping that the sale would finally ease his bitterness. If I could give him his share of the money, perhaps, he would eventually stop focusing on making my life a living hell, and become a responsible father to the children. Although I couldn't imagine going back to him, I had always wanted us to have an amicable relationship.

I was so desperate to sell the house, that each time a sale fell through, I was depressed; and each time I would again prepare the house for viewing. I would spend hours cleaning, buying flowers to create a welcoming ambience, take the children out so the house would be empty for the estate agent to do the viewing. Each time my hope would rise, hoping that this time I will finally find a buyer, but every time something would prevent the sale from happening. I would go through the same excitement, hoping that I would finally be able to move out of this house, but nothing seemed to work. I did everything in my power to promote the house to the future buyers. I was so desperate for a new start, a new house with no dark shadows, a place that belonged to me, a place I would be happy to be in.

My desire to move was so strong I went from one estate agent to another for 8 whole years, desperate to sell, but after so many attempts, so much deception and mental fatigue, it was time to give it up. It was time to try a different approach. It was time to let God take control, because

I had done everything in my power to move from this house, yet nothing had happened. So, I had to surrender it all into God's hand.

As human beings, we want to control our destiny, we want to control our future. Like me, you probably find it difficult to surrender to the higher power. I was struggling, I don't know about you, but I found it very challenging until I realized the best way forward was to surrender to Someone who loved me and like any parent who wants their children to come to them in time of troubles, God our father wants us to come to him in times of need.

"When you are in trouble, worried or sick at heart and your plans are upset and your world falls apart, Remember God is ready and waiting to share the burden you find much too heavy to bear- So with faith, 'Let Go and Let GOD' lead your way into a brighter and less troubled day."

- *Helen Steiner Rice.*

However, this was not the end. Unfortunately, the decree absolute in 2009 was the beginning of other struggles.

I was in shock, in shock over the fact that although the divorce was pronounced the nightmare was still far from over. John's determination to kick us out of the house beggared belief. Nothing could bring him more satisfaction than to know that he would finally collect his money.

January 2010 The Financial Settlement,

The Respondent Husband shall within 56 days from the date of this order transfer to the applicant wife his legal and beneficial interest in the property 45 Crambery Road London

*Subject to the mortgage secured thereon in favour of Abbey Plc on condition that as from the date of the said transfer the said property do stand charged by way of legal charge as security for the payment to the Respondent Husband of a lump sum equal to 10.68% **of the gross selling price.***

Provided always that such charge shall not become exercisable and shall not carry interest until:

- *The youngest surviving child of the family shall attain the age of eighteen years or complete her full time secondary education whichever shall be the later.*
- *The death of the wife*
- *The remarriage or cohabitation with another person as man and wife for a period of 12 months in any 24-month period of the applicant's wife.*
- *Voluntary vacation of the property by the wife's husband for a period in excess of 6 months in any 12 month period.*
- *Any dealing with the property by the wife whichever shall first occur or further order of the court and shall thereafter carry interest at 2% above Lloyds TSB Bank base rate for the time being in force. Provided that in any event the said legal charge shall not be exercisable without the leave of the court while any child of the family*

- *in occupation of the said property is still a minor.*
- *Save as aforesaid the Applicant wife and the Respondent Husband's claims for financial provision, pension sharing and property adjustment orders do stand dismissed and neither the Applicant Wife or the Respondent Husband shall be entitled to make any further application in relation to their marriage under the Matrimonial Causes Act 1973s23*
- *Pursuant to the Inheritance (Provision for Family and Dependants) Act 1975 s15 Court considering it just so to order neither the Husband nor the wife shall be entitled on the death of the other to apply for an order s2 of that Act.*
- *Liberty to apply as to the implementation and timing of the terms of this order.*
- *No order as to costs*

Following this settlement, a constant harassment, pressure, persecution started because the financial settlement wasn't clear cut. I was liable for the mortgage payment and he still had his percentage increasing as long as I paid the monthly payments.

In December 2012, I made an application for shared residence in respect of our three children. Despite my active encouragement for John to be involved in the children's daily life I felt my last resort was to take the matter to court for the judge to intervene by forcing John as the father to take up his responsibilities towards the 3 children.

It's unfortunate to say but some fathers can so easily wash their hands off the responsibility of bringing up their children. If we mothers take the same approach, who will raise the nation? We mothers often don't have the finances, and struggle to make ends meet, but yet we have to find ways to feed our children. There is no other option and we have to provide for school dinner fees, bus fees, uniform fees, mortgage payments, groceries, the list is endless. We find whatever money we need to provide for our children. It is unacceptable that fathers are allowed to leave the burden with the mothers and just walk away from their responsibilities. It's unfortunate to say, but the system allows them to do this.

What happened in court left me speechless. I was openly told by the judge that unfortunately there was nothing he could do. The judge clearly stated, 'We cannot force a father to take his responsibility; we cannot force him to look after his children."

I felt powerless, I couldn't believe what I had just heard from the judge. I looked at him and asked, "Can you please explain to me how you can force a man to pay his council tax and yet you cannot force him to look after his own children?"

I am afraid to say years later I am yet to receive his reply.

When a male Judge openly tells a man that it's ok, and they will not force him to look after his offspring then what else is there? What else could I add to this statement? I was left powerless, the Law allowed a man to openly dump the responsibilities of raising his children on the mother.

Regardless of what I said, the decision was made. He walked out of court with the Judge's permission to walk away from his responsibilities. The only justification he gave was the fact that he is working and therefore could not look after the children, I felt like grabbing the Judge and screaming at him. I felt like deserting, the court, the children, the system which allowed such injustice to go on.

God help me, I am so angry, I am so upset, how can a judge allow such a thing? This is absurd! How can he allow this man to walk away from his responsibilities? This man, begged me to have children not only one, or two but three. He was desperate to have three children, but yet here we were in court, and he was given permission by the judge to dump the responsibility on me alone. The system told him it's alright to walk away from his responsibilities.

In December 2014, I was dragged back to court, John made a claim to have full custody of our son. The absurd thing was this application was for only one child. My deep desire was for him to take care of all the 3 children and not only one. I had to attend court again.

I was dragged back into a feeling of resentment of the court scenario. Why was I being brought here again? Why does this man use the system to his advantage? This is the same man I had asked for many years to support me by taking care of all his children.

The system granted him a hearing, so here I was again, in court on the 22nd of December just before Christmas.
The children and I went through a number of meetings with the Caffcass agent to determine whether or not K

would be better off with his father. After
many weeks, of evaluation the decision
was made.

The Cafcass made the decision that K
should remain with his sisters and myself.
Bearing in mind that K had not lived
with his father since the age of 3. K's best
interest was that he would see his father
on a weekly basis but remain with us.
After a long battle, John's application was
rejected.

The after divorce felt like an untamed
bonfire consuming my heart. It ravaged
my inner strength, my peace and
happiness. John had become evil and was
determined to make me pay at whatever
cost. He threw a missile at every
opportunity he got. At every opportunity,
he would throw yet another bomb at me,
yet another missile, leaving me completely
heart broken. I sat on the stairs with my
face in my hands and hot tears running
down my face asking, "God why?" He

wanted a divorce, he was now remarried, he would benefit from the sale of the house though he didn't contribute, so why the need to be so vindictive?

Today was a bright and sunny day and the children were with their father, but my younger daughter was due to come back at 1pm to attend a Math's tuition lesson so she could get into a Grammar school. Knowing who I was dealing with, I gave her £3 to take the train and left the tuition fee on the kitchen table for her tutor. I had organized everything so I could go to my meeting. Next thing, I received a phone call from my daughter, "Dad doesn't want to let me come" she reported. My heart sank, I boiled with anger. I was on the train going for a business meeting to find an investor for my Creperie so I couldn't possibly cry. I was beautifully dressed so I had to compose myself. My heart wept, Lord when will this end? When will this father finally see what I'm trying to accomplish with his children? What will it take to be set free from such wickedness? Lord I am tired it's been 9 long years of constant attack and aggravation.

A Miracle Trip

Chapter 20

My mother's 70th birthday was coming up and my sister called, "You have to find a way to be there, I know you don't have much money but please find a way." She pleaded.

"Discipline is the bridge between goals and accomplishment".

Jim Rohn

I decided to put £50 aside for 3 months so when the time came to book I had a little bit saved. I was online trying to book the tickets, the Eurostar was £500 and I couldn't afford it.

BA flights were £400, even with my discount I still couldn't afford it so my final option was the Ferry which cost £140 for the crossing but I still needed another £100 for petrol.

Remember, regardless of how hopeless your situation may seem, please look up to God, He will rescue you. **Psalms 23. "The Lord is my shepherd, I lack nothing. He makes me lie down in green pastures, He leads me beside quiet waters."**

Later that evening I received a call from a close friend of mine who was just checking on us. Before I knew it, she had decided to come with me to Paris and was willing to help with petrol and the crossing fee. *Always turn to God, and he will make a way where there seems to be no way.*

My children's father pulled another nasty trick. He refused to give my first daughter who had been staying with him her passport, claiming that he was the one who paid for the renewal. I had her ID Card, but unfortunately it had expired so she couldn't travel without an ID or a passport. I tried to explain to her the reason she couldn't travel, but she refused to accept my explanation and because I didn't want any more arguments and aggravation before I set off, I let her come. While I was driving to Calais my mind was doing some serious overtime, I was freaking out asking God when this man would finally let me be. Though he had remarried the situation was still the same. I was busy deliberating on what I would tell the police at the border. At that moment an inner voice said to me, "Carole, God will make a way," go and fear not, don't let evil thoughts fill your mind, don't let him take away your joy. Let God fight your battle. I then remembered the preacher's message at Richmond Church, John 15:7 "The Lord says, if you abide in me and my words abides in you, ask whatever you wish and it will be done for you."

Eventually after nearly 2 hours' drive we arrived at Calais. Passport control asked us for our ID and passport. We were all sitting nervously in the car wondering what would happen.

Anxiously, I wound down the window and handed over our documents, and to my amazement, guess what? No question was asked, the only comment was, "Have a safe crossing." I leave you to imagine the relief we all felt, our first action once we were on the ferry was to give God thanks for making a way when we couldn't see a way. Always trust in the Lord no matter what your challenges are. Look up. As Les Brown once said, "If you can look up, you can get up".

After 4 days in Paris we were on our way back to the UK. We had all had a great time including my friend, and were ready to face the journey back home. Because we were returning we all felt the hardest part was behind us; so we drove with confidence and no longer worried about my daughter not having any document. Unfortunately for us, as we approached the Border Control we were asked to come out of the vehicle and were directed to another room to explain why we didn't have any legal document for my daughter. At first I felt extremely nervous and ashamed, then angry, because of what we were having to face simply because this man refused to give her the new passport. I was fuming inside, if only you could see how angry I was. I wanted him to feel this humiliation too, and how it was to be treated like an illegal immigrant with no papers just because of his vindictive action.

But once again the Lord was with me, as I was battling to keep a positive and confident mind. I was trying so hard to pray against the devil controlling my mind.

As Joyce Meyer's book said, "The mind is a battlefield, we have to guard our mind."

I can only reinforce this, whatever you are going through, your mind will be the determining factor, it would either deliver you or condemn you, it all starts in the mind.

My recommendation is:
Keep a Positive Mental
Attitude at all times.

I know it's hard, I have been there and have still not arrived yet. I still get upset and angry but I have come a long way since I learned to control my inner voice, and my wish is for you to reach this place when you learn to control your inner conversation, you learn to control your mind so it doesn't go in every direction. My prayer is that my journey will help you to become a better version of yourself. I know it's hard but do it, you can, let's try together.

So eventually through a quiet prayer, talking to myself, battling with my mind for 10 to 15 minutes, finally my peace came back. I was able to smile again and was friendly to the officer and guess what? You reap what you sow, the officer told me that he was willing to let me through but I must renew both documents immediately on my return to London. Praise the Lord!

God knew from the moment I left the house, what would happen at Calais, he was in control all the way. I now know the lesson that I had to learn. My lesson was to let go of my anger, my resentment and let God take over my heart and my mind. Next time someone is trying to undermine you or to hurt you, monitor your inner conversation and let God take over.

Education Matters   Chapter 21

*Nelson Mandela once said "Education is the most
powerful weapon which you can use to
change the world".*

"*A* quality education has
the power to transform societies
in a single generation, and
provide children with the
protection they need from the

*"Be like a
postage stamp.
Stick to it
until you get
there."*

Jim Rohn

hazards of poverty, labour exploitation and
disease, and given them the knowledge, skills,
and confidence to reach their full potential."
By Audrey Hepburn.

Education matters significantly to me
so I always do my very best for the
children by putting them in good schools,
paying tuition to allow them to pass 11 +

exams. For the past 7 years I had to face one of the worst oppositions from the children's father. I would book a lesson and he deliberately would not let them go while they were with him.

I tried to explain my vision for his own children. Although I never once received from him a penny towards tuition, yet he was still determined to make it difficult at whatever cost even if this meant sacrificing the children's future on the altar of revenge. So many times I had to pay for last minute cancellations because he just wouldn't let them go.

So, for many years on top of having to find the tuition fee, I also had to battle with someone who was happy to destroy whatever good I was trying to do.
It was as if you are building a house, you've gathered all the cement, wood, and roofing and as you start building, someone comes and destroys your work, then you build again, and they come again, and destroy what you fought to

accomplish. Each time you must find strength to build again, and each time they destroy everything and it goes on and on. But with God on your side, the enemy can't win. I would call the tutor, apologize again and keep moving. Keep supporting the children in their schooling, and finding ways to educate them.

Summer 2016
Deep Hurt

Chapter
22

It had always been a struggle with my eldest daughter. She loved her father deeply, and always craved his love and

> "If you don't like something, change it. If you can't change it, change your attitude. Don't complain."
>
> *Maya Angelou*

attention. On numerous occasions, she would disappear after school and arrange to meet with her father without my knowledge. I would never stop her from seeing him, and couldn't understand why she felt she had to sneak out to do so, and even more so I couldn't understand why the both of them couldn't be open about it.

I was constantly battling with her hurtful words and her insistence on living with her father, as if I was the one who prevented that. In her eyes, her father could never do any wrong but on many occasions she would get ready to go with him and at the end he wouldn't turn up. Though she could see how distressed I was by her father's attitude, yet nothing could ever put him in the wrong. She worshiped him, and her blind love for him sometimes made me jealous.

I was always to blame and I could do no right in her eyes. Our daily life was always a struggle because of her feelings for him. She always defended him no matter what. Regardless of what I did for her it was never enough. Nothing I could do was good enough. She was judgmental and unappreciative, I could do nothing right. She craved to live with her father from a very young age; she desperately sought his attention, his approval, his appreciation and love. No matter what I said or did I couldn't win. she constantly blamed me for every situation.

One Sunday after church, she disappeared again without my knowledge, and unfortunately her father never asked her to call me to inform me of her whereabouts. I believe somehow, he approved her behaviour and even enjoyed it. On that day, my daughter returned home around 6pm and I knew that day this had to end, I wasn't going to accept this anymore. The lack of respect on their part had to stop.

She arrived in her father's car like nothing was wrong. I calmly asked her to get all her belongings and go and live with her father that I was no longer prepared to accept such behaviour. Since neither she nor her father had the respect to call or text, or even consider that I might be worried not knowing what had happened there was simply no point any more. Of course, they couldn't understand why I was being "difficult" and why they needed to respect and inform me as a mother.

I made my decision that afternoon and I was adamant. I was extremely calm but very upset.

Eventually she realized in my quietness that I couldn't be more serious. So, she went upstairs, packed her bags and left in her father's car. I was mentally, physically and emotionally exhausted, I couldn't accept this anymore I was just tired.

Worse to Come

Chapter 23

For many months following this incident, I was blamed for throwing my daughter out. She was told everyday her mother kicked her out, and for months all I heard from her was, "How could you kick me out?" Though she was driven away in a Mercedes, I was still to blame; I could do no right. From the day she went to live with her father was *the beginning of another nightmare journey.*

"You may tread me in the very dirt but still, like dust, I'll rise."

Maya Angelou

My daughter's father made a claim straight away to the CSA for maintenance. Without wasting anytime, he called the child benefit to claim £60 and whatever other claim he could make.

I can recall receiving the first letter from the CSA.

Sitting on the floor in my bedroom, opening all my letters wishing most of them weren't bills, I wondered how I ever was going to get out of this dark spiral. Then my eyes caught sight of a letter from the CSA, I tore it open and my jaw dropped in disbelief.

How on earth could they expect me to pay for maintenance when I was already struggling to survive? I just couldn't understand how they could expect me to pay him to look after his own daughter when I had two other children at home who he didn't contribute anything towards maintaining.

I was on the floor, my body tense and bowed over. I held back tears, and fought hard to control my emotions because of my son who had come into the room. I didn't want him to see me crying. I had to control myself. I was so tired of this persecution, tired of fighting. Lord help me, how am I going to overcome, where would I find strength to fight him and the CSA? I can't afford a lawyer.

I prayed in earnest "Lord I surrender this new challenge into your hands; I am going to lay it down and let you deal with it because I just don't have the strength anymore."

I had painful images of being homeless on the streets, and there was no way out. How could I ever free myself from the constant persecution and struggles of being a single mother? Dying wasn't as hard to think about at this time, it would free me, free me from this cycle of emotional abuse, the dread of constant court summons and eminent slide into a perpetual life of poverty and depravation. I imagined how my children would be traumatised and even psychologically damaged as they faced the horrible news of my death. My mind was locked in a deep emotional turmoil, but as always my angel's voice was there to comfort me,   so I went on my knees and cried out to God.

With no support from the children's father, the pain of being a single mother with no substantial income was bearing so much on me. I was unable to meet up with payments, even though it had been more than nine years, I feel I will never be free of this heartache. I was tired of pretending that everything was alright when it was not. I don't know how much more I could take.

Going to work and school run were now becoming impossible, I couldn't afford the petrol cost. I had hoped to move but unfortunately, the house sale had fallen through again. This situation could no longer be sustained and something had to give. It would either be my children's education or my work. Besides, I was now tired of being an Air Hostess, regardless of my position as a Team Leader I was tired of a company controlling my future, and tired of working in the big Corporate company for 20 years with nothing to show for it. Years had gone by, and my finances were pretty much at the same level, I had been working on a part-time contract but I felt it was time to move on in my life. I urgently needed a change.

So, strangely one day while I was sitting on the plane, when one of my colleagues mentioned that British Airways were offering early redundancies, you can't imagine how happy I was to hear that. My heart beat with excitement, I couldn't wait to get on the ground and find out more. I was as excited as a child who had received a present that she had wished for, I could barely contain my elation, but I had to. As a manager I didn't want my colleagues to see I was happy at the prospect of leaving, this for me was a dream come true, an opportunity to let go.

So as soon as we reached the ground I made some enquiries. The lady at the office informed me that the bid had closed and I was a few days late, but I was so determined that eventually she reopened the list and gave me 48 hours to make my decision. I then went for a long walk in central London, promptly returned to the office and made my decision.

It was final, my 20 years of working as a cabin crew was now coming to an end and I must tell you I was delighted, it felt right; it was time for me to move on and so far, no regrets.

It would be the beginning of a new life, new opportunities, new directions and new experiences. While working for BA I had started a mobile crepe business so I made the decision to focus on it. I had let the excitement of being able to run my business blind me to the difficulties ahead. Not being able to receive an income no matter how small had put us in more financial difficulties and I had to rely on Universal Credit. For the first time in my life I had to go to the government for support and what an experience this was.

I felt ashamed as I walked in. My mind using the situation to put me down, mocked me quietly. How did you end up here? This is your reality now, this is your destiny, the outcome of your life. The negative voice rejoiced at my plight, the devil is always happy when we are low. I was ashamed of who I had become. I had never for once thought I would be visiting such a place. I had managed for over 9 years as a lone mother to maintain the mortgage, the bills, the children, and the house, and now here I was, at the benefit office.

As I looked around the waiting room, everyone looked dull and depressed, desperate for financial help. No one smiled and no one looked happy, everyone came with a problem. Here I was looking glamorous as usual, I made an impact, as I walked in, and from the looks I received, the people were probably wondering if I was lost.

I asked the security guard for directions, and he rudely directed me, there was no hello, no smile, nothing. I went upstairs and waited for my coach to call me. When it was my turn, I greeted him warmly, but he didn't show any interest whatsoever. His tone was dreadfully condescending as if I was a nobody. Although I was doing my very best, smiling politely, there was no reciprocation. As a matter of fact, he was rather rude, and treated me like I had been living on government benefit for years. Although I mentioned I had been employed for 20 years he simply couldn't understand that, I was only a human being who needed support rather than judgment, and I found his cold attitude very upsetting.

After this experience I understood how easy it was to stay in such a situation.

I saw how some agents treated individuals, which would without doubt make them feel like second class citizens with no importance or value. I now understood how easy it was to give up fighting for a better life, and instead settle to a life of mediocrity. I was there, but what saved me from this journey in my life was my positive mindset, my thoughts

As I walked into the Job Centre, my mind was positive. I was having a great conversation with myself "You know this situation is not here to stay, this is here to pass so don't worry, learn from this new experience you're going through." I felt confident as the stream of positive thoughts flowed "If you keep a positive mindset, you will remain focused. Don't worry about it, stay focused. Stay focused on your dream, stay focused on your goal, remain positive." I continued to encourage myself, "You must focus on the unseen, believe and you will succeed."

With these words I felt strong and was even more determined not to let this situation define who I was. I was powerful, I was successful, I could do all things through God who strengthens me. Lord you are with me; you know my heart, my desire, my dream. Stay with me, be my strength, surround me with your love. Help me to remain positive and not be engulfed by this situation.

Luke 11:9 "So I say to you: Ask and it will be given to you; seek and you will find; knock and the door will be opened to you."

Lord I am determined not to let this situation get the best of me. I am determined to remain positive regardless of what I'm going through. Lord, I do not want to stay in a situation where I have to beg the government for my daily bread, I don't want this mediocre life, a life of barely enough. Lord I want a life of abundance and fulfillment; I want a life of prosperity to be able to contribute to this world. Help me to rise from this experience, and not to stay in this situation, help me to rise above it, and grow from it. This situation is not here to stay, it's here to pass. So, as I'm going through this unattractive building with poverty written all over its walls, my mind is set because you are with me my Lord.

Deuteronomy 31:6 "Be strong and courageous. Do not fear or be in dread of them, for it is the LORD your God who goes with you. He will not leave you or forsake you."

Those profound words kept my mind spiritually strong, through the storm and helped me to remain focused and positive.

My journey through Universal Credit was a battlefield of my mind. I fought hard not to let this episode get the best of me, I could see why many might struggle to leave this mindset and way of life.

A life where you resign and stop fighting, resign wanting anything more, accept mediocrity. A place where you don't feel as important as those who are doing well, those who are in full time employment, or those who own their own business. I was here now and I could see why so many couldn't find the will to fight. It's hard to explain until you are there and you can feel it, experience it, live it.

I would often question if God had a plan for me. How can I move away from here? It's been 3 months and I can feel the impact on my mind, I could feel the humiliation every time I walked through the building, every time one of the case workers spoke to me.

Lord what's the way out of here? As you know my aim is to set up my own Creperie-Guadeloupe restaurant Bar, how can I move from here to there? Please show me the way. I am in a hole and I'm scared to stay there too long, I'm scared that I also will surrender to this fact of my life. I refuse to surrender, I refuse to accept mediocrity, I refuse to live a life of barely enough, please give me the strength to get up and fight, give me the strength to keep walking, and to keep pursuing my dream.

It was so difficult to remain positive in such a dark time, so difficult to keep visualizing your dream when the reality shows you the lack of money, the unpaid Mortgage, the house situation with everything needing repair. Although I am a very clean person, there was only so much I could do.

I looked at my make shift bed of two mattresses piled on top of each other, the duvet used as a curtain, worn carpet in desperate need of changing, the ensuite taps not working, and the shower pressure too low to have a decent bath. All these discomforts I saw. But I decided to put on another pair of 'glasses', and see the situation differently. I could now visualize the unseen. See things as though they were. The magic of dreaming big, dreaming of a better life, a better house, a better surrounding. The life I was presently living did not reflect who I was, it didn't fit with my DNA, I deserved better and I would get the best that life had to offer. I refused mediocrity, I refused the life of barely enough. And see a different world out there.

> *The universe was ready to help me to have faith, because to believe is to achieve. I encourage you, like me to have faith to call forth those things that be not as though they were.*

I once heard that money doesn't make you happy; but obviously, the person who said this had enough money to buy groceries and other basic things. I also believe money doesn't automatically bring happiness because we all have problems with or without money, but I would rather have problems with money than without it.

I went to the supermarket to pick up some groceries, and as I walked into Sainsburys, I remembered my brother who had just had his first baby boy, so I walked to the baby section to buy a little gift for my nephew. All the clothes were on 25% discount which was very reasonable so I looked around at all the different clothes and accessories for children. I was trying to enjoy this little moment of happiness but my mind was telling me "You know you don't even have £20 in your account so don't get over excited, come back to reality." At that moment, my daughter came with a water bottle she needed for school so I had to tell her I couldn't buy it although it was only a few pounds. My negative thoughts began telling me how I shouldn't look at things I couldn't afford, and how bad my financial life was. It continued to tell me how I should accept this life of mediocrity.

As I walked to the till, I wondered how I was going to pay for the bag of potatoes, the kale, the carrots and the pyjamas which I had chosen for my nephew, everything came to £13. Here I was thinking how I would pay. I held my breath and my daughter looked fixedly at the card reader. I inserted my main Lloyd's card, and it was declined. Fumbling awkwardly in my purse, I tried the Santander card, it too was declined; my last option was the business account which I wasn't sure had up to that amount. Relieved, it went through and I was eventually able to pay for our dinner as well as the gift for my nephew.

As I walked out of the store my heart was heavy, my daughter's eyes were overshadowed with sadness, no words were spoken but we both felt the heaviness and humiliation of our plight. I then realized she had taken her school shoes off. I asked her why, and she replied that it hurt because they were too small for her. I was so heartbroken all I could say was, "Perhaps you could ask your dad to buy you a new one", she looked at me sadly and I looked at her, we both knew the answer to that.

It is with great and deep sadness that I must say I have never been able to rely on him not even in those darkest moments. I received more support from friends and church, than from him.

I had tried so many times in the past to explain how much we were struggling yet he remained oblivious to the situation that the children and myself were facing. I can recall one experience when I had asked him to buy groceries for the children. The humiliation I felt because of his lack of compassion and his cold detachment towards our plight made me speechless, I would rather go to Food Bank than ask him again.

As I walked out of Sainsbury, my inner negative voice kicked in again but I was determined to push it away so I started praying, begging God to help me overcome this challenge, and to help me to make something of myself so I repeated over and over again while I was walking.

'We become what we think about.'

'I can overcome any challenge with God's strength.'

'I am powerful, successful, caring.'

'I am beautiful, rich, loving, and ambitious.'

'I deserve the best in life and I will get the best of what life has to offer.'

'I refuse to live a life of mediocrity.'

I repeated these sentences, over and over for 15 minutes until we got home; and because of those sentences, I was able to hold back my tears. I was able to go through it and grow through this situation but I must tell you, it was so humiliating not to have money for your basic needs. It puts you in a state of mind that wants to give up on life, to surrender and accept mediocrity, it deprives you of your self-respect, you feel like a nobody, a second class citizen, someone who is not worthy of living. My books, my bible, my daily devotion, my affirmation was what saved me.

Would you like to try? This might also help you if you are going through a difficult time.

Changing and Growing

Chapter 23

The children's Dad was due to collect them, and there was drama as usual. Nothing ever went smoothly He would grab at any opportunity to make my life difficult.

"Don't cry because it's over, smile because it happened."

Dr. Seuss

This time the children had a barbecue and sleepover planned, and as usual he refused to take them, claiming he would not do any running around, and if they wanted to go to the activities they should stay with me.

My baby daughter was in tears, her face marked with sadness, begging him to take her to her sleepover yet he wouldn't budge not even for a tearful littl desperate to be with her friend. Nothing could make him move, nothing could melt him.

As I witnessed this my heart was broken, I thought to myself should I keep them? But then I remembered two weeks ago he had found another excuse not to take them, so I had to stand firm and didn't interfere.

My son too was also upset and once again I was in the situation where the children wanted to stay with me purely because they wanted me to be their chauffer and do the running around, so I had to control my emotions, and say NO.

I was so sad, and felt so sorry that this was the reality. I was ashamed for having chosen such a man to be a father to my children. I was gravely disappointed in myself, how could this have happened? How did I end up here? I was so broken seeing the hurt on my daughter's face, as I drove her to school I could barely concentrate on the driving. I knew she wouldn't be herself at school, the bubbly, happy child had once again had her heart broken by her father, yet if I tell them it was best if he didn't come anymore they would be upset with me, so I resigned and watched powerlessly, there was nothing I could do to mend her broken heart.

I dropped them at school. The arrangement was that he would collect them from school, and guess what? At 4.30 my son called me, his father didn't show up, I asked him to call his father because I was sleeping. The 4 hours a day school runs drive had taken its toll on me and I was completely exhausted, I needed to rest. But what happened next forced me to surrender.

My son began to cry, begging me to come and fetch him because his father wasn't going to. I got up, quickly grabbed something to wear, then drove 45minutes to pick up my son.

What happened next showed me that I

was now in control of an unpleasant situation. As my son sat down, I greeted him with a big smile. His eyes were puffy from crying. He probably thought no one would come, and the worst part was he had already missed the last bus that could have taken him home, so I can imagine how panicked he must have been. I offered him a snack and a drink. From his expression I could see that he was relieved that I had come to fetch him, and relieved that I had been gracious to drive all the way when his father was the one supposed to pick him up, I was still smiling. I was happy to be there for him and he could see it from my facial expression

I was so proud of myself I was now in a position, where I could control my emotions. I was now in a position where my emotions no longer controlled me.

My recommendation is:
Try to control your emotion, because when you do, you will control your

action, and by controlling your action
you will control your life.

I know it's not easy, it took me many years, and I don't want you to go the same painful road, so please learn from me. I am your friend. I care about you. Control your emotions; don't let your emotions control you. You are in charge, and you must stay in charge.

Once I got to my daughter's school which was 2 hours from collecting my son, their father was there so I kissed both of them goodbye and I left them with him. They were still trying to stay with me but I had to learn to be firm. I spoke with my mind not with my emotion, and my NO remained NO.

While I was driving back home, I made the decision that my weekend was going to be good regardless of everything. I declared it, affirmed it, and owned it. Yes, I had driven 2 hours for no reason, yes, I had to get up from bed exhausted, yes I was not annoyed, yes, once again he was trying to get to me, but guess what? The new me would not allow anyone to have this power over me, so I sang, listened to music and by the time I came back my smile was back on my face and I was ready for the weekend.

I would like to ask you to do yourself a favour if you can, whenever you are facing a difficult person, tell yourself that you are more powerful. You have the power to control your emotions, repeat it over and over again. Repeat it until your subconscious connects completely with what you are saying. Repeat it until your mind no longer focuses on who or what upset you.

Let's try, for instance, if you are upset with someone tell them in your mind while you're facing them "I release all negative thinking towards you, you do not and will not have the remote control. I have the remote control and I choose which channel to press, I choose the channel of positive thinking, I am in

control so you have no power over me."
Repeat this over and over again. "I have
the remote control in my hand, and I am
keeping it, I am in control so no matter
what you say or do I am in charge of my
emotions." How did it go?

You must do it long enough to see the
result, and if you fail, do it again, and if
you fail again then do it again until you
master it. Don't worry, I also didn't get it
right straight away. Practice makes perfect
so keep practicing. Every time you are
faced with an argument, remember to
take the remote control.

My Early Life in London

Chapters 24

When the sun shines upon you

I was on a coach to London, looking forward to my holiday with my friend. I stayed at her place

"Nothing can dim the light which shines from within."

Maya Angelou

every time I visited London. She was my sister's friend, and now had become my friend also. I was so excited; although it was an 8 hour journey from Paris I was fully awake. I loved the scenery, the feeling of reaching the coast of Dover was as if I had been around the world. Each visit to London was magical.

Although the weather was always grey and misty I learned to love it. It's uniqueness, it's greenery, and everything else which made England very special to me. The people, the architecture, the diversity of the country, and the cosmopolitan culture made London unique and valuably authentic.

As always, staying with my friend was an experience. We went to church, did a lot of shopping, visited friends, and enjoyed London's beautiful scenery and attraction. I love the feeling of being in London, I was happy, very happy, and I felt like staying. I felt like a part of my future was here. So after many holidays, in 1996, I made a decision to remain in the UK. I was offered a Job with Eurostar at the time the Eurotunnel was built. It was an exciting adventure. I was so proud to be working for them, I was 21 and happy to be in London I felt peace within me, I was content. This moment of my life was total happiness. We were living life to the full; parties, holidays enjoying the freedom of a carefree and problem free life. I must admit I felt very lucky. I had a good job at the time, and was living in a very nice flat. My boyfriend at the time wasn't great, but that didn't matter. I was still happy.

During my years at Eurostar, I met John. Life was fantastic. He was very kind, loving, and most importantly persistent in his attempts to conquer me. I must admit he wasn't the type of person I wanted to date, but his perseverance and kindness made me change my mind.

After a while, I decided to accept a date. Although I wasn't passionately in love, I was comfortable. I felt secure, and well looked after. He was a true gentleman; so this was enough to gradually bring me close to him.

After few months of dating I moved into his lovely flat. Life was great. I was happy and very content.

I can still recall living in the flat; I would come home from work, and the table would be beautifully made, the meal superbly cooked. He was an amazing chef.

Some days, I would come home and find beautiful flowers all around the house, other days it would be love notes, and some other days I would find a beautiful hot bath, with rose petals scattered on the floor, dimmed lights and a nice glass of wine. It was pure magic, like living in paradise.

After 2 years of living together we decided to get married. The aim was to have a small ceremony at the registrar's office in September 1999 and have a big wedding with family and friends in July.

But July surprised us all ...

The birth of my lovely daughter was such a breathtaking and joyful moment. Giving birth was an ecstatic and jubilant experience. My daughter's birth filled a place in my heart that I never knew was empty, a new me was also born, I was a mother.

All the time I marveled, at the tiny being growing deep inside of me, turning, floating, swimming and now here she was in my arms, completely dependent on me to live, what an experience. My heart was full of love for this new little creature. Suddenly, nothing else mattered more than this little angel. She changed our lives forever; she transformed our hearts and mind.

My daughter came into a lovely environment. She was loved by two parents, lived in a very nice little house, she had a dream bedroom with light yellow furniture, and light magnolia coloured carpet, no shoes were allowed in the house. I am a very clean and tidy person so all her clothes were always nicely ironed and neatly folded. Her books were beautifully displayed on her bookshelf, and her toys were all placed in a big white box. Her room was a little fairytale room, a place of tranquility and joy, a place of peace where we didn't even talk loudly, it was a little sanctuary.

Spending time with her every day was magical, seeing the changes the progress, the little smiles, it was all amazing.

This was the time you put life into perspective, the moment when nothing else mattered, the moment that love was all you needed, a moment of happiness and pure love.

Although we had planned to get married in July, we were happy to postpone the wedding to the following year, but the following year we were hindered again by lack of funds and lack of focus. We didn't plan the wedding, and two years later my son was born.

There is a sanctity involved in bringing a child into this world, and especially in certain cultures where the birth of a boy is uniquely celebrated. I can recall that time. For weeks, the atmosphere was one of big celebration, his father was so elated by his birth, I could read the happiness all over his face. Our son's birth gave new meaning to his life. There was a deep satisfaction in his behavior and words. It's amazing how each child can bring something completely different to one's life, each birth is unique, and I could see and feel this with our son's birth.

Culture also has a huge influence in the lives of us Africans and Asians. A son represents a king's birth. It meant that the name and lineage would continue. We might not all agree to this, but it is the reality.

We were now parents of two young children, enjoying life as a new family. Those moments were unique, sharing the joy and progress of our children together brought so much happiness to our hearts. Sometimes it took a simple smile, to bring a warm and happy feeling.

When a child or an adult smiled, it lit up the atmosphere and that was very important. If in our daily lives we can smile, if we can be peaceful and happy, not only us, but everyone will profit from it. If we really know how to live, what better way to start the day than with a smile? Our smile affirms our awareness and determination to live in peace and joy. The source of a true smile is an awakened mind. Children often set this example and their smiles bring joy to us.

Often the demand on a small family can be very challenging. Nothing could have prepared us for this experience; the lack of sleep, lack of time together, the constant demand from the children. It could put a huge strain on a relationship. Although we were happy having our children we didn't expect the work involved to be so consuming. We were going through a storm, but I knew after this, the sun would rise again; I knew this situation was not here to stay and eventually the demands would ease, and so they did.

I was enjoying the family life, the joy of parenthood, with everything that was involved. I had become more relaxed and less overwhelmed by being a mother of two children.

From the day we got married John always wanted three children. I can still remember the party we had after getting married at the registrar's office. In his speech, John was laughing about it when he replied to the question about the number of children he would like. Although I was very content and comfortable with two, I decided to complete my family with three. So when my son was two years old, my second daughter was born.

After my last pregnancy I felt that I had given him the very best that I could. I felt that as a woman, I had honoured him by giving him the ultimate present a woman could give to a man. I was happy to make him happy. I felt that I had done my duty as a wife and a woman.

But yet the storm came upon us....

Now, the demands that came with having three children under the age of 5 were enormous. I knew deep down this would pass, but going through the storm was difficult. When my last daughter came, I prayed to God to give us the strength as a couple to cope with the demands of raising a small family. I prayed for wisdom and for God to make us stronger as a couple, and to give us patience towards each other while raising our family.

I could feel the increase in our costs, I could feel how money was now becoming an imperative. My expectations with regards to John were rising, I wanted him to be more ambitious, more career driven. I felt since I had completed my role as a wife and a woman I was now expecting him to fulfill his by earning more to take care of us financially. I could neither understand nor see his vision and dream for the future, I couldn't see his plan for us, and how he intended to achieve it. So because of that my respect was diminishing, my love for him was being affected, I felt insecure with having him as a leader of our family. I felt like a boat adrift on the ocean. Every woman needs security before love. Yes, love is important but primarily we need security. It can be difficult to follow a man with no purpose or vision.

A man needs to have a vision for the woman to follow.

Most women regardless of how much they earn, want their husbands to support the family and most importantly to support them. Most women enjoy the pleasure of having a husband who can sustain them. We as ladies, want to be cherished, we want our man to take care of us. Yes, of course we want to work, but I don't believe any woman wants to be in a position where she is forced to work to support the family. Wouldn't you prefer to be in a position where you can work because you want to, and not because you have to?

I am a very ambitious lady. I have always worked, and will always work, but I find great pleasure in working because I want to and not because I must or have to. I must admit since I have been a lone parent of three, I have been in a position where I have to work and I don't enjoy work as much. I am forced to work, so I do so but if I could turn back the clock, I would rather work for pleasure and not because the household are relying on my meager salary.

I truly believe God has a very clear purpose for the man.

These 3 things were given to man:

1. Work, God gave man work before woman.

2. The garden was given to man to protect and keep. This is why a man's duty is primarily to protect, provide and care for his family.

3. God gave woman to man as a companion and a helper, as we all know a helper is as strong or stronger but certainly not weaker.

The man's role in the society has changed so much that men no longer know how to be men. They no longer know how to be a provider, a captain and a leader. Some men live with no purpose; it is difficult for a woman to follow a man who does not know his destination.

I feel complete and satisfied as a woman when I am with a man who can sustain me, and provide for my needs. I feel at peace within my femininity knowing that my captain is in control of our family.

Unfortunately, the fact was he was no longer fulfilling this role, and my respect for him was diminishing. I could see myself in the cockpit as a copilot with a captain who didn't know which direction he wanted to go. I could see a captain with no clear vision of his destination.

A lost soul; and I admit that was when my frustration started to show.

I am as guilty as he is of the breakdown of the marriage. I know the lack of respect I had for him made the situation worse. My frustration was starting to show through my words, through my lack of attention to him. I loved him, but I no longer respected him; and no matter what I was trying to do, the respect couldn't be regained.

I know I was in the wrong, trying to love someone I no longer admired or respected. I was becoming a nagging wife, trying to find ways for him to improve his life. I even applied for work for him. I took the liberty to arrange a job interview without discussing it with him. I was so desperate for him to find his purpose, and to be the captain of our family that I overlooked one important thing, the fact that I was taking away his pride, I was so eager for him to come to himself I would do anything to encourage him or to persuade him to do better.

During the first year of our marriage John and his friends invested in a restaurant. He contributed £10,000 without my knowledge. You can imagine how furious I was at the fact that he said he didn't feel the need to discuss it with me as this was his money from the sale of his flat. In a strange way, I was also proud to finally be part of my husband's project.

I remember the opening as if it was yesterday. My cousin and I did most of the cooking. The food was a success, the restaurant was beautifully decorated. It was a thrilling moment. I was very proud and I felt a sense of purpose, a sense of having something to do and to develop. The customers were so pleased with the evening and we were introduced to the guests and received a lot of compliments. The night was a great success.

Few months went by and John's involvement became less and less, especially in the financial side of the business, his friend kept him away from the running of the business. I used to get so mad because I could see the friend's manipulation. I could see the lack of respect he had for John and how he kept him away from the business. This man was a master of manipulation, he knew John well enough to intimidate and disrespect him, and still pretend he wanted the best for us and our family. I disliked him so much and I often went upstairs when he came to our house.

Eventually as expected, one day out of the blues this man closed the restaurant and moved back to France and we never heard or saw him again. John lost his investment and we had to painfully put this experience behind us.

Although I was relieved that the restaurant was closed and this man was finally out of the scene, something inside me was broken. My respect was shattered.

I never viewed John the same after that. I was deeply disappointed now having to reassemble the scattered pieces on the floor. I couldn't find a way to move on, I was stuck in anger and resentment.

We had to move on and count our losses, but strangely and chokingly, John still couldn't see his wrong. Until this day, he never sincerely apologized for his lack of communication and for not involving me when he made his decision. I believe such an important decision needed to be discussed with the most important person in one's life.

Pride had taken over, and from that moment onwards, I knew his pride was going to be an issue in our relationship. I didn't know how to manage it well; I didn't know how to tackle this, and find a way to bring him out of his cave. The silent treatment was becoming more and more frequent. I would beg him to talk to me, try to kiss him, to give him attention and provoke him sexually, yet nothing was strong enough to get rid of his pride and silence. Not even looking at my beautiful face and body. Unfortunately this situation sometimes would last for weeks at a time. *Silent treatment is a dangerous poison to any relationship.*

If you are subject to this or you are the one who is inflicting it on the other party, I sincerely urge you to change, it's dangerous venom. Try your best to solve it by bed time, although it is not always easy, I know I have been there myself, but once you master this, the reward will be worth the effort, so try your best, and try again, and try again until it works.

With my life experience, I am now equipped with so much more understanding, and I'm much wiser when it comes to men. I was so immature at 21, but now, I now know and see all the wrong I did during my relationship and I pray that one day God will give me another chance to try again. If not, I am happy to devote my life to help you to save your marriage, your relationship, and your family because it's very important to me to be able to help you, I love you and care about you and your family's wellbeing.

During my marriage, my constant pushing and criticism broke him rather than build him. I was so eager to see him doing well that I overlooked his ego and I can honestly say I probably crushed it on many occasions until he probably had none left. I didn't deliberately want to hurt him but I was only trying to find a destination, a purpose, a focus for us to be a part of. I was trying to give him a vision to show him all the possibilities that lay in front of him, of us. My number one desire was to support him in his goals, in his plans, and I needed him to have one.

How difficult it is to elevate a man when you had no father as a role model. Although you want the best for him, for you, for the family, it is difficult to know how to tackle those issues especially if you never had any male figure in your own life. I just didn't know how and what to do or say. I felt powerless, and eventually we did attend mediation but the hurt was too deep.

So ladies this is my advice to you, if you want to learn from my mistakes and save your marriage.

First:
A man's ego is important to him. Learn to respect and accept his pride, value his ego as if life depends on it. Don't run him down but encourage him at every step.

Secondly:
Be part of his vision and his purpose; take great pride in helping him to accomplish his goal. By doing this you will fulfill your purpose in his life and the children will

benefit from your efforts. You will be encouraging him to excel and to strive higher. By doing this you will have a successful husband and harmonious marriage. I guarantee you will win on a much bigger scale and most importantly you will become a role model to your children and anyone else who happens to cross your path.

Third:
Men's number one priority is to have a purpose; once they do they will become the base, the head and protector of the family. Work is what makes a man, work is what makes a man feel valuable and gives him a sense of direction. Men need work and we ladies need to support them in finding this or developing it, and be a part of it.

When I speak about work I mean his purpose, his project, his business, his dream I don't mean his job, working for another man.

I recommend you to read **"The Battlefield of the Mind"** By Joyce Meyer. In her book, you will learn how to master your mind to receive the best outcome. You will learn how to talk to your mind, your inner voice before your talk to your husband or your wife. The devil will always bombard our minds with negative talk, fears, suspicions, doubts but no matter how bad the condition in your life is or in your relationship don't give up, never give up because winners never quit and quitters never win.

Regain the territory the devil has stolen from you. Regain it one inch at a time, but regain it. God will give you the strength and don't forget with him by your side you can overcome any challenge, I repeat any challenge. So let's start, step by step, inch by inch, start with a micro win and your micro win will become a macro win and eventually you will overcome what you once thought was impossible.

Be positive, because positive minds produce positive lives. You will only succeed through a Positive Mental Attitude. Start today, start now, please do not wait, don't postpone, don't procrastinate *DO IT NOW.*

Ways to Love Your Husband

By loving the man. When a man knows that he is loved, he feels secure and valued. By showing respect for the man's purpose - respect is very important to most men. If respect is shown for his purpose, it gives him the confidence that he can achieve what he has set out to do.

> "You can have everything in life you want, if you will just help other people get what they want."
>
> *Zig Ziglar*

By assisting him with the detailed tasks that need to be carried out. Most men see the big picture, while women are good at seeing the details like what it will actually entail to achieve that purpose.

By encouraging the man when things go wrong. The last thing a man wants is for his woman to nag him or say "I told you so" when things go wrong. If a woman encourages him at this point, and then makes suggestions in a humble manner about how to take things forward, the man will greatly appreciate this and will be able to continue without giving up.

Helping Him Fulfill His Purpose

One of the most important choices you will need to make is to marry rightly. This choice is so important that if you miss it, you will suffer and if you get it right you will enjoy your relationship and fulfill both yours and your man's purpose.

A bad relationship affects every area of life and hinders a woman from supporting her man to fulfill his purpose. This subject is so important that so many married women wished they had made the right choice.

The Bible speaks about whoever God has joined together! The honest truth is that God is not the one that joined most couples together but circumstances and motives.

Becoming each other's friend is the first step in the journey. There is also a God given vision in a man and often times it will require the help of the woman to help the man discover, develop, deploy and dominate his gift in fulfilling purpose.

Therefore, if you are a single woman, don't be in a hurry to get married; you have the best opportunity to prepare for it by looking for the dynamics that will help you and your partner fulfill your dreams together.

For two people to come together to live in peace and harmony, they must first agree spiritually, mentally and physically. It is important to pray for a godly man, for nothing can beat this. The question to ask is what do you need in your man and what does he need from you?

Communication is the key word. It's difficult to support what you don't know.

> ***My recommendation is:***
> *Use the time of being single as*
> *a time to improve yourself, your*
> *mind, and body.*

Develop interests, be part of various social clubs, do more than work. This time is so valuable, use it wisely; because there will be a time when you look back and miss those precious times as a single person. There is nothing wrong with being single, enjoy and embrace these moments.

True Relationship is about giving and contributing to another person's happiness. It's to be able to accept their past, support their present, love and encourage their future.

Being a Mother of 3

Chapter 26

I was in the kitchen feeding my three angels, and suddenly a feeling of responsibility grabbed me. I became nervous

"Life begins at the end of your comfort zone "

Neale Donald Walsch

and the realization that I was a mother of 3 children suddenly dawned on me. My heart thumped with an overwhelming feeling of happiness mixed with anxiety and fear. Questions rushed through my mind, would I be able to manage? Would I be a good mother and were we a strong enough couple to survive the demands of a young family? It was certainly a strange feeling, it was a combination of contentment, anxiety and worry.

As the months went by, I enjoyed motherhood but the demands were real, the lack of sleep, and lack of time together started to put a strain on the relationship. Although I was fully aware that this would pass I still had to go through it and sometimes I must admit I didn't know how to get through it.

Our last daughter was only a year old. Although I was happy to settle with two I was delighted that my last daughter was here too. I was pleased to have satisfied my husband's desire to have a third child. I felt a satisfaction of having accomplished his dream of having three children.

Getting used to being a mother of three took some time, but eventually I settled well into it. I felt an immense satisfaction, love, and accomplishment when my last daughter was born. She gave me such a deep joy that I perhaps put my husband unintentionally on the back-seat.

I was so contented with her, my inner peace was so deeply satisfied it was hard to detach from her.

When my daughter was nearly two years, we decided that I would go to Nice. It would be good for us to have a break as the relationship was going through some difficulties. Although it was my initial decision to leave, at no point did John ask me to stay so we could work things out. He never made any attempt to dissuade me from going, so perhaps deep down he also wanted a break and was happy for me to move to the South of France with the children.

The Trip to Nice

Chapter 27

John and I drove all the way to the South of France. As we arrived Nice, we drove through the Promenade Des Anglais with the beautiful palm trees along the promenade. We lapped up the beautiful scenery, the sunny blue sky and the sparkly blue sea. It was picture perfect.

"All we have to decide is what to do with the time that is given us."

J.R.R. Tolkien,

I felt joyful and content, a deep satisfaction welled up within my soul. I was happy, very happy and willing to see what the future had in store for me, for us as a couple, and for the children.

John and I parked the car, just the two of us together without the children, it was an intimate moment, and for some reason very enjoyable at this precise time, we enjoyed each other and I leave the rest to your imagination.

The unpacking was eventually finished; we collected the items and my car which had arrived separately by train at the station. The children had stayed in London with friends while we sorted out the moving. Few days later we went back to London and the children and I returned to Nice via British Airways.

We arrived Nice Airport. The children were still quite young ages 6, 4 and 2 years. They didn't understand what was happening, but were happily admiring the airport and staring excitedly at the big aquarium with all the different exotic fish. It was magical to them.

I was now in Nice, with my car, and a minimum of belonging. But I must admit that while the children were staring at the beautiful aquarium, I suddenly felt a deep sense of fear. I was worried about how I would manage this new life, although I was on talking terms with John, I was still here alone. After over an hour at the Airport we took a taxi to our lovely flat, 101 Promenade Des Anglais.

The flat was 3 bedrooms which was enough for the four of us. We enjoyed unpacking and went straight to the beach opposite our flat. It was a thrilling moment watching the children enjoying the beautiful sun, the beach, the and scenery. It was truly a blessing and although I had some fear I was also very happy. As Les Brown put it, *"Feel the fear and do it anyway."*

I have always been a very bold and courageous person and I knew somehow God would make a way and he did...Whatever happens, trust in the Lord and stay positive...

First I met Richard, who introduced me to Aida a young lady from Senegal who was willing to help with the children while she was studying. Meeting Aida was one of the best things to happen to me. Until today I bless the day this incredible, amazing girl came into my life. I am truly grateful to have met her.

Aida's primary role was to help me; she saw I was in Nice alone with three children, working as a part-time cabin crew for British Airways. I was working on a 75% contract, meaning I worked 7 days in London and had 7 days off in Nice. In one month, I would work an average of 14 days and have 14 days off, this was an ideal roster allowing me to earn enough to pay the rent and look after the children.

Working on a 75% contract allowed me to be home 7 days at a time with enough time to enjoy the children, before I went back to the UK to work. Having Aida by my side was a true blessing. I felt secure leaving her with my three children. Seeing the way she handled the children was a learning curve for me. To

Aida, taking care of three children was nothing, she often mentioned that in Senegal she had managed many more and I could see from her relaxed attitude that it wasn't such a difficult task for her. I learned to relax, to embrace the journey and most importantly to enjoy the children. Aida taught me to stay calm and manage the fact that I was alone with my children and it wasn't the end of the world. She taught me how to be a better mother and to this day, I am truly grateful to her.

Living in Nice was such a pleasure I can barely describe my joy. Every day when I woke up, I took a run on the beach. My heart would fill with contentment and joy, I felt a spiritual connection with God. I was so happy I could barely describe my happiness. Before I dropped the children at school, which was only a walking distance from our flat, we would stop at the beach for 10 minutes, throwing stones into the sea, and after the 10 minutes of relaxation, we would walk to school. The children especially my eldest who was only 6 was doing extremely well in CP which was equivalent of Reception in the UK. Although she never studied French I was amazed at how she was at the top of her class so quickly and how easily she settled. My son and younger daughter were still in nursery school, but all three settled very quickly and were all overjoyed to be in the South of France.

Seeing the children happy was a real joy for me, and I never doubted my decision. Coming to the South of France was by far the best decision I had made in my life. I can honestly say the trip saved me, because while in London I was drowning. For a whole week I would stay in my room, wouldn't eat or come out of my bedroom. I had no will to live; I was desperately unhappy and had even tried to commit suicide. I could no longer bear the life I was living. I was unhappy in my marriage, in my soul and in my being.

As the months went by I started to make friends in Nice, I went out a little and I truly embraced the life I had in Nice. I was still faithful to John, he came once every two months. We were making plans for him to join us, and I had even applied for jobs for him, but soon realized he wasn't as enthusiastic as I was to settle in France. I later discovered that while I was in Nice he had been having a relationship with someone, so eventually, his visits became fewer and fewer, and the gap between us widened even more. So I again made the decision to try a different approach.

A Different Approach

Chapter 28

Although I was very happy in Nice, I made one of the most difficult decisions in my life which I regret

"True humility is not thinking less of yourself; it is thinking of yourself less."

C. S. Lewis

to this day. I came back to the UK in order to save my marriage if it was still possible. My marriage and my children was everything to me even more than my own happiness. I learned from this never to put other people before your own happiness, not even your children or your husband.

We women always feel that we have to sacrifice our own happiness for others. I urge you to find your own happiness first if you are not doing this at the moment. I urge you to prioritize yours first because if you don't, you will eventually resent the people you are sacrificing yourself for. Often they are not even aware of your sacrifice, and sometimes very ungrateful.

My recommendation is:
Love yourself, take care of yourself, make yourself happy because only you know how to make yourself happy and you shouldn't expect anyone else to make you happy. Of course, others will add to your happiness, but it is primarily your responsibility to take care of yourself.

If I knew then what I know now, I would never have made the decision I made in 2008 to come back to the UK to save my marriage, to give the children their home and comfort. I was absolutely devastated making the decision to come back. My inner soul was sad, extremely sad. I had been so happy in France. I came back reluctantly, but for a pure and honest motive which was to save my marriage if it could still be saved. I thought I ought to give it another chance.

To my surprise what came out of this was my worst nightmare. As I arrived the UK after a year in the South of France, I discovered that the current tenant and John had come to an agreement that the house should be sold and profits shared, which showed he had no intention of working on our marriage.

Following their agreement, I had to reiterate the fact that our house wasn't for sale and while I was living in my friend's house for a few weeks we needed our house back. All 4 of us were sleeping in the lounge on a large mattress so this situation couldn't continue. Although I gave the tenants notice they were still determined to remain in our property.

So, after over 2 months back in the UK I had to find a solution to get our property back bearing in mind I didn't have John's support and his goal was to sell no matter what.

I could recall a conversation in which he clearly told me that the government would re-house me in a council flat. I leave you to imagine how devastated I was to find out that first, I had made a huge sacrifice in order to save our marriage, and John had ulterior motives.

Our return to the UK had created animosity between us. He was furious and all his actions reflected that. He became very evil. I didn't know that the darkest moments were yet to come, what I experienced on my return was worse than all the previous issues we had had. I felt as if a demon had been awakened in him.

I looked for ways to get our property back, bearing in mind that with my income I couldn't afford a lawyer. I went to a Citizens Advisor but not much help was available because I was still working part-time for British Airways. I approached Legal Aid and believe it or not years later, I was still paying the outstanding fees plus all the interest for the divorce because I didn't qualify for any aid.

Remember in life whatever happens, trust in the Lord and be positive.

I met Mr P Long Solicitor's firm who after listening to my story were willing to write a letter to the tenant free of charge asking them to vacate the house immediately. The letter from Mr P was so well structured with all the legal phrases emphasizing my entitlement as the home owner and the fact that I had three children to house, that it forced the tenants to vacate our property within two weeks of the letter.

Eventually after two months of battling with John and the tenants, we were finally able to get our house back. I leave you to imagine how furious he was. Regardless of his desire to sell, I still found a way to get our property back.

This of course meant he wasn't going to

receive any money from the sale because the house wasn't for sale. This aggravated him and the price I had to pay for his anger nearly destroyed me. But my faith saved me; with God's strength I can overcome any challenge

John became so furious, that I was in fear for my own life. His bitterness was indescribable; I felt as if I was dealing with the devil. No matter how I approached him, I just couldn't win. I can recall the time when we had nothing in the house, we slept on the mattress for many months and had no fridge or TV, most of our belongings had been destroyed by the tenants so we had to start all over again.

I was struggling tremendously, looking after the children, working part-time, paying the mortgage alone which took most of my salary and trying to rebuild our life.

I had to buy new furniture, a new bed, a new washing machine, and so on, there was no support from John whatsoever. As a matter of fact, he made everything as difficult as he could.

Settling Back in the UK

Chapter 29

Settling back was very challenging. I remember looking at the house which was in such a state. The kitchen floor

> "The greatest glory in living lies not in never falling, but in rising every time we fall."
>
> *Nelson Mandela*

was full of food stains and I knew no matter how much I cleaned it the floor would have to be stripped. The cooker looked as if it hadn't been cleaned since the 6 months the tenants had been in the house. The washing machine was not working. Each bedroom was saturated with damp, the windows had probably never been opened. The carpet as you can imagine, desperately needed changing. It was covered with dark marks and greasy footprints. Everywhere looked revolting. The house needed a complete makeover.

Fortunately, I was still working part-time for British Airways so I was able to buy new items every month, and gradually we rebuilt our life. It took us between 6 to 9 months of sleeping on mattresses but eventually we made it.

I can recall the times we would sit on the mattress watching a film on my phone because we had no TV, computer, or radio, those moments of closeness were unforgettable they brought us closer together.

Those moments showed how resilient we were and how we could all build and start again as long as we were willing to face the challenges of life. With a positive mental attitude you can overcome anything.

After a few months we were now settled back into our house, but the challenge of childcare was one of those things I am glad I won't have to relive. Au pairs were my main support throughout. Some were not great, some were fair and others were great, and some like Aida were amazing.

Aida knew how to take care of the children, cook, clean, and how to play with them. Often she was much better than I was, because her focus was on them while mine was on either paying for the house, the bills, or sorting out the school fees, meals, or uniforms.

> **My recommendation is:**
> Although you are busy providing for the family and bringing in an extra income even if you are a lone parent you should still set aside a day once every week or two to dedicate 100% of your time to your children. Because before we know it, they are no longer children who need us but they are children with deficiencies, children who seek attention because they lacked it.

Chapter 30

Growing up with my mother and my 7 brothers and sisters was fun. Our early years in Guadeloupe was magic.

> "*Success is the ability to go from one failure to another with no loss of enthusiasm.*"
> **Bob Proctor**

Living in Guadeloupe with its amazing scenery was truly beautiful.

At the age of 10, we all moved to Paris after the tragic death of my older brother in a car crash. We lived in a very small 2 bedroom flat in Paris. I can still visualize my bedroom. It was no more than a little corner with a bunk bed, but my corner was always immaculately tidy, my bed sheet well spread, and cute fluffy teddy bears sat around my bed. I was always very particular, clean, classy and chic according to my family who nicknamed me "Madame."

Nature was our daily blessing, the landscape, the waterfalls. Our town was a tourist destination because of the scenery. The splendid greenery attracted people from all over the world, and sometimes we sold mangoes, bananas and passion fruits to tourists for pocket money. It was an ideal childhood.

The only major issue in my childhood were my mum's words. Her words were like venom, dangerous harmful poison. Her words could cut like a knife. Those words could have killed me and caused me to do all the wrong things in life. I can still remember her words:

"You will never amount to anything."
"You will be nothing but a drug addict on the street like your father."
"You are ugly, look, at your big lips."
"You are dark and unattractive."

I was constantly insulted, smacked, and

humiliated. I was always told "look at your dark ugly big lips". I must say after all the insults and humiliating words, God still blessed me with a pretty good look.

During my teenage years and all through my adulthood I was determined not to let my mum's words be true. I was determined not to let her poisonous words define me. I made up my mind to succeed; I was hungry for a better future. Because of that, and thanks to her, I kept away from drugs, alcohol, prostitution and any other wrong doing.

My mum's words were so engraved in me that for many years I had to pray to undo the damage those words had caused me. I had to work on my mind, work to rebuild myself, I had to mend my broken heart, find the good in me, and discover why I love me, Carole. So, I embarked on a journey to improve myself, through reading, writing, learning anything which would help me empower my mind. I discovered Toastmaster public speaking and fell in love with it from the first day. I decided that my words would be used to empower others, build confidence in them, encourage them to build their self-esteem and their ability to accomplish great things.

> **My recommendation is:**
> Don't let anyone's words define who you are and who you must be.

Words can be venomous, a dangerous poison, but words can also mend a broken heart. So, let your words be warm hearted and most importantly loving. I know from my own mistakes it is not always easy and I have made many mistakes myself but I urge you to choose your words carefully.

We have all been hurtful with our words, so before you speak, think about how your words might affect or hurt someone because once they are said, YES they can be forgiven BUT they can never be forgotten. So, let us all use our words to empower others.

Gun Raped

Chapter
31

You can overcome any challenge with belief.

O n a bright and sunny afternoon after dropping all my belongings in my new room, I was on my way to Argenteuil town center, France to buy a few kitchen utensils for my delightful newly acquired little bedsit. I was excited to finally be leaving my mum's house just like any other 20 year old looking forward to being independent and becoming their own person. I was looking forward to discovering the wonders of life.

"He gives strength to the weary and increases the power of the weak."
Isaiah 40:29

I was at the bus stop but somehow after almost half an hour there was no bus coming. Suddenly this car stopped at the bus stop and the driver asked me "Would you like a lift?" I was feeling uncomfortable but he was very persuasive telling me he also was going to town and waiting for the bus on Sunday could take long. I got into the car and sat nervously beside the driver, but he felt this so he tried making me comfortable by asking general questions such as "How long have you been in this town?" "Where are you from?" I replied very politely with an innocent smile, "I'm from Guadeloupe the French Caribbean, I just moved to this town and I am looking for kitchen utensils." He replied that he was from Africa and I nodded.

While driving for perhaps 20 minutes I tried to figure out where I was. There were a lot of tall buildings. We went under a bridge and finally into a car park where he had agreed to drop me. To my horror his face suddenly changed. The kindly man had become a monster, a dark beast. I tried to open the door to run, but he quickly locked the door and commanded me to look at the back seat which was covered with a cloth, as I lifted the cover I was visibly shocked at what I discovered, guns, perhaps 4 or maybe more guns. I then realized I was in danger. There was nobody in the car park, nobody to help me, the car door was locked, and I had a gun to my head, "Shut up and be quiet! It won't take long." He barked. Tears streamed down my face as I was raped by this monster. Realizing that I was still a virgin, he had the audacity to ask if I had a boyfriend and how come he hadn't slept with me yet? I was numbed, frozen with fear, my thoughts were in disarray. This can't be real, what is happening to me? Oh God, what is happening? Is this a nightmare or reality? Is this man raping me? Lord help, please Lord help, help, help.

I was broken and scared that he was going to kill me, what can I do to stop this? Oh Mamam please come and help me I am being raped and no one around to help. I was imprisoned in a car with no escaped route, I tried to push him away, but I was weak compared to him so I eventually surrendered. I cried, my heart was racing, my world had collapsed, I was in total confusion. Is this happening? Is this real? He then opened the door and threw me out. Humiliated, scared, dirty, broken inside me, I made my way to the nearest police station.

As soon as I entered the police station the team could see by my distraught face and my disorderly clothes that something terrible had happened. They sat me down and gave me a drink of water, left me for a while and returned to take my statement. I tried to recall what had happened and at that moment it was as if I had been hypnotized, I couldn't remember the car, the man, the town we drove through, the car park we went into. It was all a blur I was in shock and was having a mental block. Eventually I was able to give the description of his face and age, I also mentioned that he had guns in the car and he was African, but that was all I could remember.

I was struggling to describe my attacker, struggling to understand if this nightmare really happened. I was completely spaced out from shock. I tried to remember through the trauma. Eventually when I was able to give a brief description of the scene, I was offered hypnotism to help me recall the moment, but somehow my conscious and subconscious wanted to erase this moment as though it never happened.

Following the ordeal, the lack of details made it very difficult for the police to trace the monster. Years went by, but they still weren't able to catch the man. I went through months and months of darkness. My life took a dark plunge. I had no will to live, to fight, or to see anything positive in life. I went through deep depression, tried to commit suicide. I just couldn't see the light to live. My experience with a psychologist did not help, so after a few months, I decided to move abroad and this was the beginning of my new life in UK. I share my life experience with you. hoping I can add value to your life, that I can bring positive support to you and can somehow help you to believe that you also can be a winner, you also can move pass the pain you are going through, you too can also achieve whatever you want to achieve. You also can move beyond any trauma you've experienced. Yes it will be difficult, I can't even find words to tell you how difficult it will be, but you can win and move forward in life if you decide.

When all around you is darkness and you can't find any reason to fight, when everything that can go wrong goes wrong and you can't find the will to get out of bed;

> **My recommendation is:**
> *move abroad, move to a different town, move house, change your job, do something, anything, just make a drastic change in your life.*

and you will discover that behind the dark room there is another door to a better room, a better and brighter future. Remember, if I managed to survive, so can you. I am not stronger than you, I am just like you. I just refused to fail, I just refused to give up that's all. So join me, keep fighting, keep moving because life is like a line, and we are all walking on that line, sometimes we fall, but as long as we get up and stay on the line of life, we'll get there. So your objective is to stay on the line and I know you can if you believe you will.

I know by the grace of God you can overcome any challenges. Repeat this everyday "I can do all things through God's strength." "I can do all things through God who strengthens me."

Declare it when you wake up, when you are having breakfast, when you are driving, when someone upsets you in the office, at home and when your husband or wife pushes you to the limit. When your children are acting crazy and infuriating you, engrave this sentence into your conscious and subconscious mind and you will reap the benefits, I guarantee you. Try it!

Overcoming Forbidden Love

Chapter 32

You also can overcome forbidden love, you can control what seems to be the uncontrollable, you also can take control of your action if you become disciplined in your mind and action.

A friend of mine had been in this situation for over 8 years and every time I see her she tells me she will end it but somehow this seems stronger than her. It seems as if the situation was controlling her rather than her being in control of the situation.

> *"God is our refuge and strength, an ever-present help in trouble."*
>
> *Psalm 46:1*

I looked at her and was thinking to myself she's a stunning lady, intelligent, mature, and very elegant. As I looked at her I couldn't understood why she chose to settle for second best, a married man.

Why should such a glamorous lady hide the man she loves? In 7 years they were only able to go on holiday once and this was purely because he happened to have had a business trip abroad which fit in with her time off and everything else around his other life. As I looked at her I could see through her, the pain, the embarrassment, the shame. It was almost as if she was in denial of how much she was trapped in this love, the feeling of being in a cage and not knowing how to escape.

I could feel the heaviness in her heart as she explained why she couldn't spend Christmas, New Year, Easter and other important dates with him. Her eyes glazed over with emotion, her throat quivered, she was fighting so hard to hold back the tears, but I was powerless. No matter what I or anyone could have done or said, wouldn't have made the slightest difference because she herself was no longer in control. Until she decides to regain control of the situation and take charge of her life, no one could help her, only God if she was willing to ask for his help.

I looked at her, thinking to myself, God I hope I will never be in such a situation. Guess what? Two years later, this amazing person walks into my life in the least expected way.

The more I got to know him the more respect, admiration and love I felt towards him. I could hear my heart beat, and feel my pulse rising. There was an immense sensation of wellbeing, a feeling that takes you on a ride to an unknown world, a flight that transports you to a different world, a different sphere than you had planned for your life. A place where you never imagined you would be. My heart would tell me I want to be with him but my mind would chide me and remind me that I can't.

How could I control myself, how did I let my emotions take over? I was trying, and trying, I didn't want to give in. Lord please help me to overcome the temptation, help me to rise above this challenge.

His kindness, his simplicity and his manly ability to handle me as a lady made it difficult to resist him. His ambition and values were remarkable. How were we going to master our inner emotion and control the situation rather than let the situation control us? I have often heard that with God we can overcome any challenge, but I never had to overcome my own flesh, my own desire, my own mind. God please give me strength, how was I ever going to overcome this?

I decided to become very busy, engaged in my daily prayer, my daily reading, I kept my mind focused on God. I had to fight, fight the temptation. There were times when during my reading, I could feel my mind drifting, I could feel the emotions rising even when I was reading the word of God but as Joyce Meyer mentioned in her book, "The

Battlefield of the Mind" which I was reading then, we need to learn how to take control of our mind if we don't want the mind to control us. But I can honestly tell you, that taking control of my mind was one of the hardest things I had ever had to do, because no matter how hard I tried, my mind, my body, my feelings were craving for him. It was so painful, so difficult.

Controlling my emotions, was so challenging, the pain was so deep at times. Craving for someone is a very powerful feeling and can be extremely painful, have you ever experienced it? Can you remember the indescribable deep pain?

I had to learn to stay focused on one task at a time, which was my reading and I immersed myself totally, I continued reading and eventually I could read one page without being distracted by my thoughts. From time to time I could find myself drifting, so I would talk to myself and say "Carole, that's enough! Focus on your reading."

As the days went by, I was able to anticipate my mind before it drifted, and I would quickly make a conscious effort to remain in my book, in God's word. BUT IT WAS HARD, VERY HARD. IT'S EXTREMELY HARD TO FIGHT THE FLESH. I had to be disciplined.

I believe our thoughts can be the most dangerous poison, but also the most wonderful and powerful thing. If we understand and learn how to master our mind we can reap a good and prosperous result.

One of the things I did was to recite this quote by TD Jakes every time I felt low. Those words became my strength to help me through challenging situations. As the day and weeks went by, I become stronger in my emotions, I was able to control my mind and chose to stop thinking about the things I didn't want to think about that did not help me to move forward, so I had to help myself. Perhaps you also want to give it a try.

My recommendation is :
There are people who can walk away from you... let them walk. I don't want you to try to talk the person into staying with you, loving you, calling you, caring about you, coming to see you, staying attached to you... Your destiny is never tied to anybody that has left. It doesn't mean that they are bad persons; it just means that their part in the story is over. And you've got to know when people's part in your story is over...

Stop watering things that were never meant to grow in your life. Water what works, what's good, what's right. Stop playing around with those dead bones and stuff you can't fix. Its over...leave it alone! You're coming into a season of greatness. If you water what's alive and divine, you will see harvest like you've never seen before. Stop wasting water on dead issues, dead relationships, dead people, a dead past. No matter how much you water concrete, you can't grow a garden. Stop trying!

By reading the word of God every day, reading positive books and most importantly, praying for strength I found that my mind was becoming stronger, I found that these challenges no longer seemed insurmountable. I felt I could overcome the mountain if I abided in the Lord and surrendered all to him, and I did reap the fruit of all my hard work. Before I knew it, I could control my mind, actions, and desires. I was becoming disciplined in my thought life and you can too.

How to Improve and   *Chapter*
Have a Better Life   **33**

Do you want to transform your life and your thinking so that you can transform your

> "The key to success is massive failure."
>
> Thomas J. Watson

future, and the future of all the people around you? Those are the questions I've asked myself, and those are the questions you need to ask yourself. Think about it, you have the power to do that, but to enable you to achieve it, you must start with the mind, you must start with a positive mental attitude which will lead you to action, and persistent action will lead you to your goals.

During the storm, I had to keep pressing on, keep on believing. Although everything around me was pulling me on every side, the negative side, the side that said, why are you fighting? Give up, let go, it is not worth it. Why do you bother? Look around you, but I had to find a way to get up each time, I had to find strength to keep on, keep pressing on and you also can overcome any challenge if you keep on fighting, keep on getting up, and never surrender. I know it is not easy I am not here to judge you, I am not here to tell you I am better, I am not here to tell you that what you are going through is not difficult. No, I am here to say, don't give up the fight, life is a fight, a fight for your territory, so keep fighting, keep pursuing your dreams, keep your daily prayer, feed your mind with God's words, feed your mind with positive thinking.

I woke up one morning, the sun was shining, I was healthy, I had three gorgeous children I had every reason to be happy yet I still could feel the negative side of my life. The negative thinking was trying to take control of my day, reminding me, the fridge broke down, we have no washing machine, mortgage not paid for the past three months, not much to eat, creditors calling me all weekend, Barclay's, Santander. I was over my limit, and because all my bank accounts were overdrawn, the bills came back unpaid,

Each day I would wonder what to give the children to eat the next day. I lived on the edge, my main priority was petrol to get the children to school and food, most especially food and I was eternally grateful to the Foodbank and all the workers for their immeasurable support. I don't know what I would have done without their help, but yet, It was very difficult for me. Each time I went the negative thoughts would flood my mind, "Give up the fight. This is your reality. This mediocrity is who you are and who you will always be." The action of going to beg for food destroyed something inside of me, it made me feel angry to be at such a low level in my life when the children's father was less than an hour away.

This action brought rage, resentment and bitterness to my heart, because this man begged me for three children and yet where is he while we are starving? Where is he? Where the hell is he? I could feel all those negative thoughts rising up, I could feel them overtaking my mind. I could hear the voice telling me that I was never going to make it. I would always have this way of life, this mediocrity, a life of barely enough. I could hear that voice.

I am sure like me, the negative voice may talk to you and often try to capture you in the morning so that it will take control of your day. So, I urge you to kick that thought to the kerb. I urge you to do like me, switch off the negative voice, use your hand if this helps you, but switch it off and switch on the positive side and keep it on all day.

During the day, the negative voice will come back to haunt you again, because it wants to win, it wants to take control of your mind, and finally bring you to this place of low morale, low self-respect, low self-recognition and low self-pride. Every time it comes, kick it out, push it out. Do whatever that can help you come out of the wilderness and move to a safer place. During the course of the day, guard your mind, protect it, stand right in front of the door and do not let the negative voice in because you and I know it's purpose is to rob us of our joy, so stand firm and guard your mind.

Being a Lone Mother

Chapter
34

I had patiently waited to be married, have a good job, a nice car, and a nice home before I embarked on the motherhood journey. Yet here I WAS.

" Whatever choice you make makes you. Choose wisely."

Roy T. Bennett

For many years, I rejected many offers to have children because in my mind I knew what I wanted and what I didn't want, and I made sure I had children when all the dots lined up together. But guess what? Life threw me out of my boat, I was suddenly in the ocean having to swim, learning to swim against the currents and trying to overcome all sorts of weather challenges. I was scared;

overwhelmed that this ocean was bigger than me. How would I manage? How was I going to take care of three children on my own? I'm scared, overwhelmed. Lord what is happening, haven't I done all that was expected of me? Where did I go wrong? Please tell me because I don't understand how I got here, I had been so cautious. I was so upset with myself for allowing love to blind me into having three children. I was upset with myself for the choices I had made.

This unfamiliar place in which I found myself had filled me with such anxiety and fear, that I struggled to remain positive, struggled to believe it will all work out. The hurt was not only that I was now on my own with the children, but the biggest hurt and disappointment was the feeling that I had let my children down. I never wanted them to be part of a toxic broken family. Their interest should be protected first and foremost. I tried very hard to shield them, minimize the impact of being torn between two worlds.

How could I shield them, when their father was uncooperative? He jumped at every opportunity to hurt me.

My heart would bleed every time I had to go to a school play on my own, I would look at all the other couples and feel like the odd one out, the typical single black woman stereotype, and often I was the only woman of color. I felt so ashamed all those years, I felt humiliated when I met other ladies and often the first question was, "What does your husband do?" A constant reminder of my situation, those questions would cut me like a knife so what do I say, do I lie, or do I tell them the truth?

Often I had to tell the truth to avoid any unpleasant and uncomfortable situation following a lie. Very often the reaction would be "Ohh poor you." So because of those comments I would refrain from going to certain places, especially if I knew it would be a gathering of couples. For example, my daughter's school organized an end of year ball and I desperately wanted to go, but because of who would be there and the type of surroundings I didn't go.

It was so humiliating walking into a room full of parents alone. It was so humiliating to be a single mother. People often define us by our status but as Lisa Nichols wrote, "Do not define me by my status, I am Lisa. Who happens to be a single mother." Those lines helped me to press on and gave me the courage to accept the situation and move forward.

Even going to church had become embarrassing. For a while I didn't want to go. As I am walking into the church with my three children, everyone's eyes would be on me wondering where is her husband? Why did she have so many children? I could sense the tongues wagging. It was painful when I was asked, "Where is the father?" It was like being cut with a knife. I would feel hurt and be bleeding on the inside, all I wanted to do was to burst into tears, but I had to face it, and present a calm and relaxed face but within I would be hurt, broken and angry. I felt like shouting. Leave me alone! I didn't want to be single, I didn't want to be a mother and a dad, God didn't design me to be a father, and a mother too. I don't know how to manage it all, but somehow I managed it and probably better than you all could have, so leave me alone with your questions because unless you are in this position you will never feel my hurt, you will not see my tears, so please stop asking me, what does your husband do? Where is your husband? Let me be! He is gone and is not coming back and as you can see I now have to manage the load, I now have to deal with it and press on so if you want to help, just offer your support and don't ask me those questions which make me uncomfortable. These were the words I felt like screaming out to anyone who asked.

Everywhere I went, I felt awkward and ashamed. Ashamed of my situation, and of being a lone parent. I was ashamed of walking surrounded by my children with no father. It was so unbelievably painful. But simultaneously I also felt proud of my accomplishment because with God's strength I was able to:

- Enroll them in private school, yes I do receive some support from the school, but I am still proud of my accomplishments.

- I was able to pay the mortgage for over 10 years alone and provide a stable home for the children.

- Occasionally I would treat them to a nice restaurant.

- The children were always nicely dressed; being French it was part of the culture to dress smart and elegantly.

- I was able to give them a Christian background, the good thing was they all liked going to church.

- My three main goals for the children are to equip them with a good education, a genuine faith in God, and finally last but not least good manners.

So, I believe I did the best I could despite my situation. I was proud of what I was able to do alone and sometimes looking at my friends who had husbands, I didn't envy them. I heard what they were going through and I was happy to be just me with my children no adult challenges at home as I was the only adult to make the decisions.

Challenges as a Lone Mother

Dealing with the repair and maintenance of the house was also a big problem. As a single lady with limited income I had always two challenges:

No1 Was to pay them for the repairs but often I couldn't afford to pay their full price so I had to ask for a discount but this wasn't always possible especially if what needed to be done was very minor, like a manly touch. A DIY person still wanted at least £100 to come to you regardless of how small the job was, and I could understand that, but often, I didn't have this money available.

No2 Was those who came and then realizing I was alone would try to receive the payment in service, they would try again and again to take advantage of my situation. It's unfortunate to say most did, only few were responsible enough to remain professional. Once I called a gardener to cut the grass because my lawnmower broke down. The first few weeks he would come and do the job, but sometime I couldn't pay him. As soon as he realized I needed his service but I was struggling to pay, he started to text me, inviting me for a drink, as I read his text my stomach churned. He felt that because of the fact that I was a single mother and struggling he could push his luck. As I read his text, I cried to God please take me out of poverty, take me out of this mediocre life. Because of my situation these men don't respect me, they see me and my struggle and want to turn it to their advantage. Tears rolled down my face as I read the text. I suddenly became angry with the children's father, how could he have left me in such a situation where I am continually fending off men?

It was upsetting that because I wasn't married they felt they could disrespect me, but unfortunately this is the way it is. Men would often think they could flirt with me and keep their nice family cocoon at home. A few had good intentions to help, but the others' motives were sex and sex only and I kept away from them. I became more resilient, and more determined than ever. I realized I was the only one who could rescue me and if God decides to give me a partner, he would find me one on my way to my destiny.

I was also lucky that somehow God had blessed me with a beautiful look, shape and body, I was very grateful to be extremely elegant and pretty for a mother of three.

Some days I would be very happy with the look God blessed me with and other days I will resent it for attracting the wrong type of men. I was very popular among men and I knew that men were attracted to me primarily for my looks, but there were those who got to know me, and often commended me for being a very good mother.

Yes being beautiful is a great thing but it can sometimes turn to our disadvantage. Stay with me and I will tell you why.

I was once asked by a man, "Where is your husband?" I replied "I don't have one, why are you asking? His reply will forever stay in my mind, "How come such a beautiful woman like you is single? You look as if you have a husband who takes good care of you for you to look so stunning and well groomed". I must admit this was the first time I was proud to be single, because without a husband I did look after myself very well, and yes I did look as if I had a husband to care for me so I did a pretty good job for myself after all. Somehow, I could be as chic as any other woman who had a husband earning well enough to look great. I was proud of myself for the woman I had become, I was proud that I had looked after myself so well, especially when others thought that I had a husband who earned well enough to take care of me. I was very proud of my accomplishment. Well done to me, against the odds I did manage very well.

My recommendation is:

You are the motor, you are the driver, the No1. So no matter what you are going through look after yourself first, God created all of us single at the start of our life and all of us will die single, but for now look after yourself. You will then have the power, the energy, and love to look after others this includes

your children, your family, your friends
anyone you come across.
So, take care of yourself.

Regarding Divorce

Chapter
35

Society views singleness as a sign of weakness, a sign of disadvantage, someone who has a problem that needs to be fixed or someone who hasn't been able to hold onto a relationship, as if this is the most important thing in life.

"Shoot for the moon and if you miss you will still be among the stars"

Les Brown

But let me tell you it takes two to get married, but only takes one to break the union. One person can't get married but one person can get a divorce.

Since 2006, the government made it even easier for people to divorce. Anyone could hide under the grounds of "Unreasonable Behaviour" which is the one my ex-partner used without even understanding the meaning of the words.

Unreasonable Behaviour can include a wide range of behaviours, from serious incidents of domestic violence and infidelity to refusing to help with the household chores. By having these grounds, it meant any one could easily get a divorce, unfortunately those rules do not support God's plan for the family. Those rules are put in place to demolish God's plan with regards to the union of man and woman. I agree in some cases that divorce is necessary but having a law which devalues marriage will not help our society.

Journey to the Top of the Mountain

Chapter 36

My journey to the top of the Mountain, what an amazing experience... join me

I am at the bottom of a Mountain and on my way to the top, as I look up I can see the top.

> "You are never too old to set another goal or to dream a new dream."
>
> *C. S. Lewis*

It's an amazing and beautiful breath taking view. I am so excited; I can barely contain my joy and excitement. I am in a hurry and can't wait to get there. I can already feel the joy of having accomplished my dream, my goal, and my purpose.

I don't know how I will get there but I know this is where I am aiming at. I don't know how but I believe somehow God will make a way for me, somehow the how will unfold as I climb towards the top of the Mountain.

I am so excited at the thought of reaching the top, I am so happy just thinking about it. I am enthusiastic and ecstatic I can barely contain my joy, I am also a bit anxious, and scared, but most importantly extremely determined. I want to feel what it is like to reach the top of the Mountain. I want to know what it feels like to have accomplished my dream, a dream to have a life of abundance, a life of success, a life of accomplishment - and purpose, to reach my goal, my heart's desire. I want to feel what is like to dream big and reach the top of the Mountain, stand at the top and look down, smile and tell myself I have done it, I have accomplished my dream. I set up Creperie-Guadeloupe Restaurant/Bar and it is a success!

But before this, let me take you to my daily routine. Before I start my journey to the top of the Mountain, I equip myself with development courses, books, public speaking courses and anything else which can help me to climb to the top. I equipped myself with good contacts, positive people, I decided to only surround myself with OQP (Only Quality People). As Les Brown once mentioned if you hang around with losers you will become a loser, but guess what? If you hang around with successful people they will eventually pull you up. Your surrounding has everything to do with your success.

Surround yourself with positive, successful, hard working people so you can learn from them and aim higher. You deserve the best so go and get the best before life passes you by.

For many years my self-esteem was attached to man's opinion. I have noticed that ladies are more vulnerable to low self-esteem than men because we are more emotional. Many of us ladies allow men to control us because we are looking for our self-esteem from our relationships or marriages.

> ### *My recommendation is:*
> *Look for your self-esteem through your relationship with your Creator, God.*

Now that I finally understand that I have been created by God, my Creator who loves me unconditionally, I have learned to love myself. By loving myself I now possess very strong self-esteem.

You need to do the same. Love God, love yourself. As you build your self-esteem, you will be able to love others more".

My Daily Devotion   Chapter
34

No1 - Every day I wake up around 5am- 5.30am. I have my daily prayer; this has now become my ritual.

"Do not allow negative conversations to be the start of your day."

Carole Bacame

A moment with God, keeps me grounded, it keeps me humble and most importantly allows me not to feel overwhelmed by my struggle. It gives me hope for a better and brighter future. Perhaps you would like to try this for a month. Wake up every day and before you do anything, eat, check your phone or emails, start house work or anything else spend the first 30 minutes praying, and being grateful for another day, another opportunity to enjoy life, another opportunity to be with the people you love, another opportunity to enjoy the simple things in life and whatever makes you happy, thank God for giving you another opportunity to redefine your priorities, your purpose, your life vision.

No2 I spend 30 minutes to an hour reading, I read something positive every day, I mean every day. It's my Vitamin, my booster for the day. I very rarely read the newspaper, I used to read the paper every day for 20 years while I was still working for BA because it was there free to read and this was everyone else's routine. So without even thinking I too had adopted this bad habit. I remember sitting in the galley, with my meal and my newspaper like everyone else did, and I would read again, again and again all the stabbing, the killing, the fraud, the evil in the world and I would feel completely deflated, dark and hopeless afterwards.

The sad thing was we didn't even read the best papers but the trash, those papers that only emphasized on the drama in the world, the papers that deliberately want to feed us with the drama, the gossip, of life. Those papers that do not add any value to our life but on the contrary take away our inner joy, by feeding our mind with all the bad news in the world. Unfortunately, they feed us on what we, the public, ask for which is even worse. The more we are fed on negativity the more we want and buy the sordid stories and the drama, without realizing the damage these newspapers are doing to our mind, soul and inner peace.

The human creature is a very strange creature, we are comfortable sticking to what we know, what we are used to, so any change will require a huge effort.
We are creatures of habits, but change is a major step which must be taken to enable us to move to the next level of our life. We must avoid habits which could be very destructive to our mind and destructive to our inner peace. If you want to change your life, you must start

by changing what goes into your mind, you must guard your mind, protect it as if it's the most precious gem you will ever find on earth, because it is.

The pictures the negative news brought to my mind were dark. They made living equal to murder, rape, fraud, killing, stabbing, unfaithfulness, divorce, pedophilia and many more deplorable things. No wonder I couldn't see the positive side of life. No wonder I was willing to accept mediocrity as if this was the best I could wish for. No wonder I couldn't move forward in my life. Yes those are parts of life, but if you look on the right side you will see that life is not only sordid drama.

If you want to be successful in your marriage, in your parenthood, in your work place, in your goals, in your relationship with God, in everything that you do, it all starts with the mind and I am not saying not to watch the news, I am saying don't feed your mind for hours and hours on it. Of course, it is very important for you to be aware of what is going on around you and in the world we are living in, but don't dwell on it, don't make the dark news the subject of every conversation you start, don't animate it, don't feed into it, because you become what you think about. Don't allow those negative conversations to be the start of your day. The way you start your day is crucial to your success, it's crucial to the energy you are going to give out to the universe.

I am sure there are far better conversations you can have, than the number of people killed in the latest terrorist attack, the last teenager murdered, our last pedophile scandal, divorce scandals and so on.

Hear it, acknowledge it and move forward, continue along your positive route, don't be distracted by the drama of the world. Stay focused, stay positive, stay connected with your goal.

The way you think in the first few hours of the day will determine the type of day you are going to have, your thoughts will set the tone for your day, it will attract positive or negative things into your day. Everything starts with you, you are the determining factor, you can be in control of the wheel, you don't have to let the car drift, don't let your life drift, take control, take charge, you are powerful more powerful than you can ever imagine.

Since I discovered that, I have transformed my life. It doesn't mean that I no longer have problems, no, life is full of problems, we all have challenges regardless of our stature, background, nationality and age. We are all equal when it comes to problems and challenges but what matters is how you approach your problem, your attitude towards your challenges and your thoughts, all those will determine if you are going to grow through it or just go through them.

My aim and prayer for you is for you to **grow** through what you **go** through, just like I did and I'm still doing every day. I haven't arrived and I don't think I will, because life is a constant learning curve. We never stop growing and never stop improving, it's an amazing journey. Come and join me on the flight to self-improvement.

No3 I am on this journey, it's exciting, amazing and most rewarding, I am so happy, I never knew that after working for over 20 years for a company that one day I will be on this journey. I had always had it at the back of my mind to explore life, and I knew I was always very driven and ambitious, and wanted much more out of life, but to finally be on my way there, and experiencing what I am experiencing is truly fantastic, words cannot explain my joy.

I am on this journey to the top of my mountain, I am on this journey to realize my dream, my purpose. I absolutely love the new me, I embrace my struggle and I can honestly tell you it is not easy to walk into a benefit office asking for help, and having to go to Food Bank for the basic need of life which is food. Receiving calls every day from all your creditors, it's not easy to dream big knowing that you are late in your mortgage payment and not knowing how you will buy the school uniform or how you would pay all your debt. It is not easy to still dress up beautifully when you don't have much in the bank account. One thing I realized during this hard time is you don't need money to look nice. I can certainly tell you that you can look a million dollars if only you know how to dress, how to present yourself, remain clean and chic and most importantly how to smile and be elegant regardless of what you are going through because a smile will elevate all the clothes you are wearing, a Positive Mental Attitude will bring beauty you never knew you had.

Why don't you try it? This month decide to upgrade your dress code, be clean and smart, pay attention to how you look then leave the house looking immaculate and face the world with a smile and a PMA and I guarantee that you will reap the reward. You will feel amazing, and how you feel and see yourself is how others will see you and feel towards you.

What I also did to improve myself was to stop asking, "why me?" I have stopped feeling sorry for myself and accepted my life as it is. This was the best decision I made for myself.

This journey has been one of the most challenging in my life, but also the most rewarding. Trust your struggle, it will bring you to your dream. Trust your struggle, it will redefine you and upgrade your inner person. Trust your struggle, it is the only way to get through to the other side of yourself, to the unknown, it will lead you to what GOD designed and created you to be.

If you would like to contact me directly to get more information about my work, or if you would like me to attend any public speaking for your organisation or event feel free to contact me on carole@carolebacame.com